Fayetteville Free Library

How to Remember Anything

3/12

Fayetteville Free Library
300 Orchard Street
Fayetteville, NY 13066

To my wife Zoe for your inspiration and belief, you are my lucky star

And for my three boys Zachery, Elijah and Noah, whose creativity and fun knows no bounds.

Teach®
Yourself

How to Remember Anything

Improve your memory and progress your career

Mark Channon

Hodder Education

338 Euston Road, London NW1 3BH.

Hodder Education is an Hachette UK company

First published in UK 2011 by Hodder Education

First published in US 2011 by The McGraw-Hill Companies, Inc.

This edition published 2011.

Copyright © 2011 Mark Channon

Database right Hodder Education (makers)

The *Teach Yourself* name is a registered trademark of Hachette UK.

All rights reserved. No part of this publication may be reproduced, stored in a retrieval system or transmitted in any form or by any means, electronic, mechanical, photocopying, recording or otherwise, without the prior permission in writing of Hodder Education, or as expressly permitted by law, or under terms agreed with the appropriate reprographic rights organization. Enquiries concerning reproduction outside the scope of the above should be sent to the Rights Department, Hodder Education, at the address above.

You must not circulate this book in any other binding or cover and you must impose this same condition on any acquirer.

British Library Cataloguing in Publication Data: a catalogue record for this title is available from the British Library.

Library of Congress Catalog Card Number: on file.

10 9 8 7 6 5 4 3 2 1

The publisher has used its best endeavours to ensure that any website addresses referred to in this book are correct and active at the time of going to press. However, the publisher and the author have no responsibility for the websites and can make no guarantee that a site will remain live or that the content will remain relevant, decent or appropriate.

The publisher has made every effort to mark as such all words which it believes to be trademarks. The publisher should also like to make it clear that the presence of a word in the book, whether marked or unmarked, in no way affects its legal status as a trademark.

Every reasonable effort has been made by the publisher to trace the copyright holders of material in this book. Any errors or omissions should be notified in writing to the publisher, who will endeavour to rectify the situation for any reprints and future editions.

Hachette UK's policy is to use papers that are natural, renewable and recyclable products and made from wood grown in sustainable forests. The logging and manufacturing processes are expected to conform to the environmental regulations of the country of origin.

www.hoddereducation.co.uk

Typeset by Cenveo Publisher Services.

Printed in Great Britain by CPI Cox & Wyman, Reading.

Contents

Acknowledgements   viii
Meet the author   ix
In one minute   xi
Introduction   xii

Part 1 Foundations

1   Memory   3
      Your memory   3
      Memory types   4
      Making connections   10
      The art of memory   13
2   The learning cycle: Take control of your memory   15
      Sense → Integrate → Act   15
      Emotion and motivation   19
      Priming your senses   20
      Framing your learning   20

Part 2 A new way of thinking

3   Creative memorization: Unleash your
    true memory potential   25
      Memory and creativity   25
      The creative state of mind   28
      Core skills   29
      In practice   37
4   Reference stories: Making information memorable   40
      Encoding   40
      Decoding   41
      Dialling up   45
      Active daydreaming   46
      In practice   48
5   The chain method: Build your capacity to remember   52
      Link by link   52
      The principles   54
      Building the chain   56
      In practice   59

6 Memory networks: Your limitless mental storage systems   61
     Classification   61
     Chunking   64
     Networks   65
     In practice   74
7 The number system: Learn the value of remembering numbers 81
     What's in a number?   81
     A new vocabulary   82
     Temporary or permanent   90
     In practice   91
8 Mind mapping: Create, capture, consume and communicate   96
     Mirror the mind   97
     Mind maps and you   99
     How to mind map   100
     The four Cs   104
     In practice   109
9 Reading strategies: Double or triple your speed   111
     Benchmark   111
     Purpose and direction   112
     10,000-foot view   113
     Double your speed   114
     In practice   118

Part 3 How to remember

10 Lifestyle: Master your memory   123
     Immersion   123
     Things to do   124
     Names   125
     Directions   133
     Physicality   136
11 General knowledge: Sowing the seeds of knowledge   139
     Sowing the seeds   139
     Geography   140
     Entertainment   142
     History   147
     Literature   150
     Science and nature   153
     Sports and leisure   156
     In practice   160

12 Programming to remember: Take control of your memory   163
    The past: Where did I put my keys?   163
    The future: Don't forget the milk!   166
13 Information overload: Strategies for remembering   169
    Emails and social media   169
    Documents and articles   172
    News   174
    Books   175
    Conferences   180
14 Delivering your message: Word for word   184
    What's the story   184
    Presentations   185
    Scripts and speeches   187
    On the hoof   191

Part 4 Progress your career

15 Agile learning: The key to continuous development   195
    The need to grow   195
    Agile learning: What's inside?   196
    Your ritual   202
16 In business   207
    Hard skills   207
    Soft skills   209
    Scenarios   211
    Interviews   221
17 Your career plan: Design your life   224
    Your purpose   224
    The plan   226
    Mindset   229
    Final thoughts   230
    Index   233

Acknowledgements

My thanks to Victoria Roddam, Helen Rogers, Althea Brooks and everyone at Hodder Education for the opportunity and support; Phil Poole for his last minute, tasty recipe; Stephen Mear for choreography that I still remember and can talk about after ten years.

There have been several people in one way or another who have shaped my thinking around memory. Thanks to the unstoppable Steve Rogers for introducing me to the world of memory techniques in the early '90s; Mel Gordon for a book that influenced my early days as an actor and informed my ideas around memory improvement; James E. Zull for writing a book that made a shift in my approach to training and coaching; Tony Buzan for his early and ongoing inspiration in the area of Mind Maps; Anthony Robbins for his strategies that have created massive change many times throughout my life.

Thanks to everyone who offered the use of their photos and the ones we were able to print: Cola Richmond, Alison Shepherd, Carol Williams, Caroline Marsden, Emmalene Evans, John Norris, John Pasonage, Joseph Pitcher, Nathan Amzi (contact@amziphotography. co.uk), Tom Kershaw, Mark Stuart, Rebecca Thornhill, John Barr, Rebecca Lock, Steven O'Neill, Lorraine Chappell, Dermot Keaney, Stephen McCarthy and Nick Brownlow (with an extra thanks to Nick for his help with research).

Thanks to Mum and Dad for their never-ending belief in all my endeavours; John and Paul for their constant support; and I have to mention Dominic for the couple of conversations that got me going – you know who you are.

With special thanks to my wife Zoë for her unparalleled support, research, ability to appear interested at 3am and invaluable motivation throughout the writing of this book.

Meet the author

It is fair to say that in my youth, I would not have been regarded as having the best memory. After training as an actor in the late 1980s I always felt fairly comfortable learning scripts; however, trying to retain names, facts and semantic knowledge was more of a challenge.

It wasn't until my early 20s after a good friend of mine, Steve Rogers, loaned me a memory course that I had what you might call 'a light bulb moment'. I have seen the exact same reaction from hundreds of people since, the thought slowly forming in their brain, working its way down to their mouth before blurting out, 'Why did no one teach me this at school?'. I was hooked; however, I wanted to do more than just remember lists, I was hungry to find out where I could apply these techniques in my life.

Around a year later while working in the West End production of *Crazy for You*, I had an interesting call from my agent asking if I had any good ideas for a game show. Being an actor, you never say no: 'Let me think about it and get back to you.' This seemed like an opportunity and within 30 minutes I wrote a format for a game show called *Memory Masters*: ordinary people from all walks of life performing incredible memory feats after attending an intensive memory seminar. Within one week of posting it off, I pitched to a production company, and in 12 months it was a weekly prime time show on the BBC, presented by Bob Monkhouse.

This started my journey as a trainer and coach in the world of memory techniques and mind mapping. Over the course of the next year, I came sixth in the World Memory Championships and was ranked third in the world as a Grand Master of Memory. My focus, however, was not so much on competition but on where these techniques could add value in a person's life.

Over the last 15 years, as well as being an actor, hypnotherapist and coach, I have run seminars for organizations such as

Rothschild, Lincoln National, Dyslexia Scotland and the BBC in Memory, Mind Mapping and Creativity; worked with students of all ages and trained at many top independent schools in the UK such as Eton, Roedean, Oakham, Woldingham, Oundle, St Bede's, Whitgift and St Peter's (York); and most recently as a Product Manager for the BBC, delivering personalization and social features for online products such as iPlayer, News, Sport and the 2012 Olympics.

My passion and experience across a mix of careers have allowed me to pull together simple and highly effective strategies in 'How to Remember Anything' that are focused on helping you progress your career and identify ways of using the ancient art of memory techniques in order to add real value to your life, be that for business or leisure.

At the core of *How to Remember Anything* is the 'idea' not just to remember but to remember with a purpose and not just to understand but to take action and get results.

I have been lucky enough over the years to teach these strategies to students and professionals of all ages and it is truly exciting to have the privilege of sharing these strategies with you.

Mark Channon

www.howtorememberanything.co.uk

In one minute

The Greeks invented memory techniques 2,000 years ago. They called them the Art of Memory. *How to Remember Anything* brings these techniques up to date and demonstrates how you can use them to enhance your life. It is divided into four parts: *Foundations, A new way of thinking, How to remember* and *Progress your career*.

Part one asks the question, How does memory affect you? Understand the building blocks of memory and how to prime yourself to remember. Discover the learning cycle and be open to sensory information, reflect on it with your current knowledge, question and take action to attain your purpose.

Part two unveils the core of memory improvement, creative memorization, and constructs your mental toolkit. It guides you through basic and advanced memory concepts, exploring how they work and how to use them. This should all be experienced through the lens of the learning cycle as your imagination takes you on a journey of the memory systems of the mind.

Part three takes the skills and strategies you have learned and uses them to guide you through a series of scenarios. You learn to use creative memorization to memorize names, increase your general knowledge, program yourself to remember future tasks, remember books, scripts, presentations and more.

Part four looks at ways you can apply the strategies you have learned to real situations, helping you further your career by being the best you can be at interviews and in your current or future roles.

Introduction

Interestingly, in the beginning I never really considered myself a 'memory guy', memory techniques were part of what I did. While I enjoyed the process of training to a high standard, competing in various championships and experiencing first-hand the positive impact that these techniques can have in many areas of your life, for me, memory improvement was always a means to an end. I think that sentiment still runs true and it is why I have been passionate about sharing the ideas in this book.

There have been many memory improvement books written over the years and I have read quite a few of them. When starting out, the thing that I looked for in most of those books was examples, 'How do I put this into practice?' This was a challenge and although there were some excellent books that gave a great insight into how memory techniques worked, I always felt there wasn't enough guidance in real-world application and enough to chew on that would allow me to immerse myself so it became second nature.

Having an eclectic background and various careers (dancer, actor, developer, trainer, coach, product manager), it always seemed clear to me that to really understand something you have to experience it and take some form of *action*, to master something you have to immerse yourself in it. Through that mastery you can perform at a high level and create the changes you are looking for in your life.

I wanted to learn how to improve my memory so I could learn scripts more quickly for auditions, understand programming when I started developing websites back in the late 1990s, memorize names in meetings, remember key facts about people, consume information from conferences, put together presentations and memorize them at high speed, programme myself to remember things at a specific moment in time – the list goes on.

Almost from the very beginning I was so excited about what was possible I couldn't help but talk to people about these amazing techniques and try to figure out how memory techniques could help them.

To that end the learning strategies and memory techniques throughout this book will take you on a journey from understanding and experiencing through immersion in the techniques to choosing how you can apply it to mastery in your own career.

This journey has four destinations:

- ▶ **Foundations** – The ideas you learn in this section will set you up for how to approach the strategies throughout the rest of the book.
- ▶ **A new way of thinking** – This is your toolkit; here you will learn your craft.
- ▶ **How to remember** – An opportunity to immerse yourself in the application of these strategies.
- ▶ **Progress your career** – Make an real impact in your career, bringing these skills to your everyday life.

The book is packed full of **Action boxes**. When you see an 'Action' box you should switch from passive reading to active participation; this will increase your understanding and memory of the chapter as well as your ability to look for opportunities for where to apply the strategy or concept in your own life. All Actions have a **Time limit**: this is the set time for each Action. While some can be completed more quickly and some take longer, the time limit constrains the amount of time you spend on each Action to make sure you keep the momentum up through the book. Everyone is different so these are a rough guide. If you find you haven't completed an 'Action' within the time limit, either come back to it later or run the time limit again.

Depending on your mode at the time, you may choose to do the Actions as you go through the book and treat it as a training session or make notes on the Actions that capture your interest and come back to these later. Even if you feel an 'Action' isn't particularly relevant, you should read through and think about where you may apply this in your own life.

Try one now: each 'Action' consists of a short game or exercise to complete.

Action – Your purpose

Time limit: 10 minutes

▶ Without thinking too hard, answer these questions (if you have a pen and paper, write them down):
  ▶ Why are you reading this book?
  ▶ What do you want to get from it?
▶ If you haven't done so already – preview this book (take no more than five minutes); flick through and get a sense of what it's about. Certain areas will catch your attention: notice these but don't focus on remembering them.
▶ Make sure you do the above steps before reading on.
▶ Make a few notes about anything you remember that caught your attention, this could be as few as one or two things or as many as 20.

You already have the potential to remember anything you put your mind to. Since you are reading this book you are probably looking for ways to improve your current ability to remember or get some practical ideas about how it can help you in your everyday life, business or career.

Some of you may only want to become competent, extracting the key techniques that will allow you to do specific tasks. Others may want to go deeper, acquiring the ability to become effective on a personal level and use the techniques in your career.

You may want to achieve a level of mastery that is integrated throughout your life, where you no longer think in terms of techniques but it's just what you do, how you learn, how you act and how you lead others.

There is no magic wand and although you will be able to memorize more quickly, remember more and retain it for longer, like any skill, mastery takes time and dedication.

The aim of this book is not to give a detailed view on 'how your brain works' but rather to offer you memory techniques and learning strategies that will add real value in your life and in your career. The intention is not to have you remember 'everything' you read or have done but to offer you the skills to remember 'anything' you put your mind to.

Memory techniques are very personal and will be interpreted in many different ways. Your goal should be to take what you read here, experience it and make it your own.

Whichever path you choose, the strategies in this book can help you make a difference in your life and your career. Have fun and enjoy the journey!

Part 1

Foundations

'Efforts and courage are not enough without purpose and direction.'

John F. Kennedy

1

Memory

In this chapter you will learn:
- *the importance of memory for you*
- *the most common types of memory that people refer to*
- *the building blocks of memory*
- *about the art of memory.*

The purpose of this chapter is not to give a detailed view of the brain but to let you reflect on the importance of memory in your life, the various types of memory you may be familiar with and your own capability. By making a 'shift' in your perception and therefore your beliefs about what is possible, you can start to unblock any pre-conceived ideas about the practical uses of memory techniques.

Your memory

It seems that in our current world, where we are expected to remember more and more, there should be more focus on not just the 'what we remember' but also the 'how to remember'. We spend years learning to read and write and months or years learning to play a sport, but when it comes to learning, and specifically to learning techniques that can help with this, the commitment can be minimal. This may be because those techniques are not readily available at the right time or there could be a presumption that it wastes time or it's easier just to press on; maybe there is a belief that it's how you are wired: 'You can remember this but can't remember that.'

Memory is an art and like any other art it takes time to master; like most things you master, the benefits can be great. The trick is figuring out what level of mastery you need to get to in order to achieve your goals. How good do you need and want your memory to be? To answer those questions you need to identify how your memory currently helps or hinders you in your life.

> ## Action – Memory in your life
>
> **Time limit: 10 minutes**
> We all inherently know that memory is vital in order to function; without memory we have no understanding or context. Answer the questions below to identify some areas
>
> ▶ Where does your memory let you down?
> ▶ Where does your memory perform well?
> ▶ If you have used memory techniques before, how successful were they?
> ▶ If you have used memory techniques before, what was the biggest challenge?
> ▶ What do you expect to be able to do after reading and working through the actions in this book?
> ▶ On a scale of 1–10, how would you rate your current memory?
> ▶ On a scale of 1–10, where would you like your memory to be?
> ▶ What does 1 look like for you and what does 10 look like?
> ▶ Make a note of your scores and put it somewhere visible.

Memory types

There are lots of different terms used to describe various types of memory. Our aim is not to give an account of all the different memory types and meanings, or whether one term should be used over the other, but rather to give an overview of some basic terms in use, giving you some context as to where or how you might experience them. This pragmatic approach will give us a common language to refer to.

Concise Learning and Memory (John H. Byrnes, 2009), references the fact that Tulving (2007) identified 256 types of memory.

EXPLICIT (CONSCIOUS)

With explicit memory there is a conscious effort to recollect, whether you are thinking about a past experience or some type of factual information.

Action – Study the following words

Time limit: 5 minutes

1 Spend the next minute just studying these words. Think about what they mean to you.

Tree	Co-ordinate	Connection
Stem	Cerebellum	Fornix
Heart	Satellite	Ghost
Medulla	Thalamus	Amygdala
Feeding	Control	Elephant
Pons	Hypothalamus	Hippocampus
Movement	Reptile	Professor X
Midbrain	Limbic	Cortex

2 Cover the words above. Look at the list of words below and identify any words you have just studied.

Fish	Pons	Medulla
Cortex	Cerebellum	Amygdala
Movement	Thalamus	Limbic
Midbrain	Reptile	Hippocampus
Fornix	Ship	Love
Dinosaur	Pirate	Hypothalamus
Cerebellum	Awesome	Remember

This is one example of explicit memory where you have made a conscious effort to recall.

IMPLICIT (NON-CONSCIOUS)

Implicit memory covers several different types of memory that are all considered non-conscious, i.e. you are not making a conscious effort to recall the information, experience or skill.

Action – Fill in the blank

Time limit: 2 minutes
Take a few deep breaths and clear your mind. As you breathe slowly count down from 10 to 1.

As you look at the following stubs of words, without thinking about it say the first word that comes to mind. Do this at speed. If nothing comes straight away, move on and come back to it. Write each word you come up with down on a piece of paper.

For ___

Lim ___

Po ___

Mid _____

Cer _____

Amy ____

Hip _____

Tha _____

Cor ___

Med ____

Hyp _____

Ele _____

Although slightly contrived in this situation, since you have previously been primed with potential words for the above stems (Med – Medulla, etc.), there is a higher probability that this will be one of the words that come to mind. This is called the priming effect.

Whereas explicit memory is conscious recall, implicit memories are related to non-conscious recall. An example of explicit memory would be being primed for the list of words above; implicit memory is knowing how to drive your car, dance or play a sport.

SHORT-TERM MEMORY

In order to keep something in short-term memory, you need to rehearse it in your mind, a new PIN number, for example. With repetition you will be able to transfer that number to long-term memory. Pure short-term memory tends to involve things you don't have some knowledge of (e.g. a phone number). In most cases you will be performing a task that involves manipulating information in your short-term memory while reflecting on information in your long-term memory. This mix is generally known as working memory, 'as short-term memory merges with longer-term memory and experience' (*The Brain: A Neuroscience Primer*, Richard F. Thompson, 1993).

Action – Remember this...

Time limit: 30 seconds
Remember this number:

7 8 2 1 6 3 7 4 9 5 3 1 8 0 1 4 2 0 3 9

Write down as many of the digits as you can remember in sequence.

Time limit: 10 seconds

Remember this car registration:

BD02 GYU

Unless you are already versed in some form of memory techniques you will probably say this number over and over again as previously mentioned, trying to keep it in your mind through rehearsal. If you happen to get distracted while trying to memorize or recall, it will be hard to keep it in your mind. Most will be able to remember seven numbers, plus or minus two, and without rehearsal short-term memory will last a short amount of time.

In *The Brain: A Neuroscience Primer*, Thompson refers to case studies where people were prevented from rehearsal by counting backwards from 10. The length of time a short-term memory took to decay without rehearsal was about 10 seconds.

Insight

You could think of short-term memory as one of those aquadoodle mats with water pens. If you haven't seen one, it is basically a drawing mat for kids. You fill a special pen with water and as you draw on the mat the water from the pen makes a colour come through. Like short-term memory whatever you draw fades away unless you keep on going over it. Although an aquadoodle mat may last longer than your short-term memory, it's a nice image to remember how it works.

LONG-TERM MEMORY

Long-term memory is used to cover many types of memory and there are several ways to classify this. We will take a broad view and look at it from the perspective of Declarative (explicit) and Non-declarative (implicit).

Declarative – Knowing that/what (Explicit)

Declarative memory and explicit memory are sometimes used interchangeably. Declarative memory includes 'knowing that Shakespeare wrote Hamlet', 'knowing what you had for breakfast yesterday' or 'knowing what ingredients make up pancakes'.

Declarative memory is understood fairly well. In 1953 a patient referred to as H.M. had part of his brain removed that included an area of the brain called the hippocampus due to suffering from severe epilepsy. After having surgery, he was still able to remember events and facts from his past. He also still had the ability to remember a string of digits up to the point where he was interrupted. He could also form new implicit memories by being able to perform tasks that were taught to him. However, he could not remember learning to do so. The fact that he could not create new declarative memories led scientists to believe that the hippocampus played an essential role in forming these types of long-term memories. We can break declarative memory into episodic and semantic.

EPISODIC MEMORY

Action – Where have you been?

Time limit: 1 minute
Answer the following questions and write down some key words that capture your answers:

> ▶ What was one of your favourite holidays?
> ▶ What was the last film you went to see?
> ▶ What did you have for breakfast yesterday?

Episodic memory relates to experiences or events that are time-tagged and include spatial information.

SEMANTIC MEMORY

Action – What do you know?

Time limit: 1 minute
Answer the following questions and write down your answers

> ▶ What is the name of the author of the Harry Potter books?
> ▶ What is your partner's or family member's birthday?
> ▶ What does mnemonic mean?

Semantic memory is about your knowledge of facts. This could be the elements of the periodic table or knowing that *karova* is Russian for 'cow'. One of the differences between episodic and semantic memory is that semantic memory is not time-tagged to a specific event: you will know that Rome is the capital of Italy but you will probably not have an experience linked to that.

Non-declarative – Knowing how (implicit)
Non-declarative is a label grouping various different types of non-conscious memory including:

> ▶ **procedural** – knowing how to dance or drive a car or play a sport (motor skills)
> ▶ **priming** – as in the implicit memory test you completed where you received the information (in this case certain words) prior to seeing a stem of those words that resulted in you non-consciously recalling some or all of them
> ▶ **conditioning** of responses – e.g. Pavlov's dogs, where they were conditioned to salivate when they heard a bell ring
> ▶ **skills** learning.

Bryden (2007) refers to Baddeley (2001) on working memory as a type of memory used to hold information for short periods of time while it is being manipulated. This also encompasses the idea of short-term memory. The picture of working memory involves a central executive that manipulates the information and three storage components:

- the phonological loop (subvocal rehearsal)
- visuospatial sketchpad (visual and spatial information)
- the episodic buffer (information retrieved from long-term episodic memory).

Working memory is essential in evaluating and making decisions.

Action – A working memory story

Time limit: 3 minutes
To help remember this model of memory you might imagine yourself as an executive in a large office. To your left is a phonogram. You turn it on and it starts playing the same words over and over again. In front of you is a large canvas with a map of your home town. You paint pictures on different spaces. To your right there is a large HD TV with DVDs that capture episodes from your life. As the executive, you can use these three resources to work with and store new information.

Read this through two more times, letting the images come to mind.

Close your eyes and recite the main points.

Now write down Baddeley's model of working memory.

This is a small taster of creative memorization.

Making connections

The building blocks of who we are were apparently discovered by accident after a section of brain was knocked into a petri dish with silver nitrate. It lay there for two weeks before it was found by Camillo Golgi, who with the aid of a microscope was able to identify what is referred to as the neuron. The neuron is the basic information-processing unit, making possible our understanding, memories and behaviours (Diamond, Scheibel, Elson, 1985). There are over 100 billion neurons, interconnected and making up what we refer to as the structures of the brain. Greenfield (1997) uses the analogy that there are over 100 billion trees in the rainforest: this is equivalent to the number of neurons in the human brain, and the number of connections those neurons can have is comparable to the number of leaves on those trees. A single neuron can have between 5,000 and 10,000 connections, a potential quadrillion neuronal connections (Sprenger, 1999). This image gives a clue to the vast potential of the human brain.

To picture a neuron in its basic form, you can break it down to the cell body (soma), the tree-like branches (dendrites) sprawling away from the soma in search of incoming information from other neurons, and the longer trunk (axon) looking for other neurons to communicate with and send signals to.

As you look at a neuron, you will see there are many dendrites and only one axon. Signals are sent through the axon and are received by the dendrites. Signals can also be received by dendritic spines (the small spines on the dendrite), axon to soma, axon to axon, dendrite to dendrite and soma to soma (Diamond, Scheibel, Elson, 1985).

Figure 1.1 A neuron.

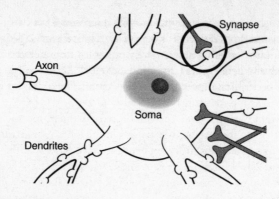

Figure 1.2 A neuronal network.

The purpose of the neuron is to transmit information to other cells. The neuron communicates with other neurons through chemicals reacting and producing electrical signals. As these 'signals' are passed on, the neurons create networks. In real life these networks represent how we perceive the world around us: a particular set of neuronal networks will fire when we try to remember the name of the person standing in front of us; neuronal networks will be constantly firing as you read this book. The amazing thing about the brain is that neuronal networks can change; a particular neuronal network that fires every time you get up to talk in front of people, making you nervous, can be interrupted and changed. If you change the network, you change the behaviour.

As the axon splits into smaller fibres, they end at the axon terminal. When a fibre makes a connection with another cell, it is called a synapse. Between the axon terminal and another neuron or its dendrite is what is called the synaptic cleft (a small gap). In order for a signal to cross over the gap, it needs help from a neurotransmitter, thus the signal can continue on. These signals are constantly firing across the brain.

The art of memory

Memory techniques have been with us since the ancient Greeks over 2,000 years ago. In Frances Yates's non-fiction book *The Art of Memory*, she tells the fascinating story of memory techniques throughout the ages, beginning with Simonides of Ceos who, after giving a poem in honour of his host, a Thessalian named Scopas, was given a message that two men were waiting for him outside. Upon leaving the banquet hall, he found there was no one there. At that moment the roof collapsed and killed everyone inside.

As the bodies were indistinguishable in the rubble, relatives who came to identify them could not recognize them. However, Simonides remembered where everyone had sat by the fact that each person was at a particular place or location and was able to guide their family to them. It was from this experience and the realization that his memory of the guests was connected to the place where they had sat that gave him the reputation as the inventor of the art of memory. The techniques that grew from this point were passed down through the ages from the Romans to European tradition, going on to give particular focus to Giordano Bruno and his works on memory.

Techniques that allow for the storage of a huge range of information are perhaps even more relevant today, in a world where information comes at us from every angle and a multitude of sources. Having been passed down through the ages, in current times these techniques are mostly recognizable through memory experts but are rarely thought of as something which could help children at school or in a business context. As we move forward, you will recognize that there are many opportunities where you can utilize some of these age-old traditions in a modern way.

While this chapter has focused on types of memory, neurons and inside the brain, it has also been an opportunity to prime yourself with some basic creative memorization concepts. Depending on how actively you participated, you will potentially remember the story about working memory and the story about the brain. Even if you don't, some ideas will have set seed and will grow to support ways of thinking in subsequent sections of the book.

KEYS TO A GREAT MEMORY

▶ Identify how good your memory is on a scale of 1–10 and how good you would like it to be (you will reference this at the end of the book).

▶ Explicit memory is conscious (remembering the capital of Ireland or the last movie you watched); implicit memory is non-conscious (riding a bike).

▶ Priming as in implicit memory test: you receive a set of words, for example, some time prior to a scenario where you say the first thing that pops into your mind after seeing a stub of that word, Ele_____. This is the result of non-conscious recall of the word. If you thought of a big creature with a trunk, it's because you were primed for this earlier in the chapter.

▶ Short-term memory needs to be rehearsed: you can store between five and nine items and without repetition it will decay in around 10 seconds.

▶ Working memory allows you to manipulate information within your short-term memory and work with information in long-term memory; it enables you to evaluate and make decisions.

▶ Declarative (explicit) memory is about knowledge (semantic) and experience (episodic). Non-declarative (implicit) memory is about learned skills such as driving a car (procedural) or buying a particular cereal from the supermarket because you have seen it that morning in an advertisement (primed).

▶ The information-processing units of your brain are the neurons: they make you who you are, allowing you to understand, remember and act. There are over 100 billion neurons, each with a possible 5,000–10,000 connections.

▶ Signals are passed between neurons, sent via the axon and received by dendrites (signals can also be received by dendritic spines, soma and axon).

▶ Simonides of Ceos was renowned as the inventor of the art of memory.

▶ There are huge opportunities to use our understanding of types of memory and the art of memory in our modern lives.

2

The learning cycle: Take control of your memory

In this chapter you will learn:
- *the learning cycle and how you can use it*
- *using reflection to create understanding and memory*
- *the benefits of questioning your learning*
- *how to complete the loop through testing your thoughts and ideas*
- *how to prime your senses.*

Sense → Integrate → Act

In James E. Zull's book *The Art of Changing the Brain*, he explores and suggests a method for teaching that utilizes research into experiential learning by David Kolb. Zull uses his knowledge of biology and experience as a teacher to demonstrate the usefulness and application of the learning cycle and how it maps to the way our brain works, how we learn and how it can be used as a model for teachers to improve learning for their students.

The subject itself is extensive, and the purpose of this chapter is to explore the learning cycle model from a high level in order to identify how it can be used to frame techniques in later chapters.

At the most basic level, the learning cycle works on the premise that we receive experiences through our senses, we integrate those experiences into our thinking by reflecting on what we know, associating with our memories and ideas, questioning and abstracting our own ideas, then complete the cycle by taking some form of action to test what we have learned.

The learning cycle is not set in stone. Numerous cycles can happen simultaneously. This is our natural process of learning. Different people will play with the learning cycle in different ways. Some might come up with great ideas and follow through on them yet claim to have a poor memory. Others will have the ability to remember lots of facts but not really comprehend and be able to put what they remember into action. Each of these types will be focusing their efforts more on one area of the learning cycle than another.

Understanding and being aware of the learning cycle can give us the opportunity to be more effective in how we learn and more importantly how we use what we learn.

Action – Explore the learning cycle

Time limit: 5 minutes
Whether we are aware of it or not, we are continuously learning. Throughout our lives, some of those lessons will have a positive effect and some a negative effect. Below is an illustration of the 'idea' of the learning cycle.

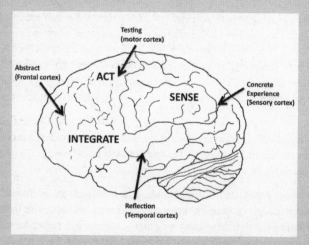

Figure 2.1 The learning cycle.

Complete the following actions:

- ▶ Study the learning cycle diagram.
- ▶ Think about what it reminds you of: what does it mean to you, what images or words does it spark off in your mind?
- ▶ Think about how you might utilize this cycle to comprehend and remember something of importance to you.
- ▶ Now write down your thoughts, or draw a picture, and either explain to a friend what you think it means or explain it out loud to yourself.

By running through the above four steps you have just gone through the learning cycle. As previously mentioned, we are constantly running a number of cycles, taking in new sensory information, reflecting on what it means, abstracting our own ideas, reflecting on those, taking some kind of action to test them out, receiving more sensory information and so on.

Let us look at each section of the learning cycle in more detail.

Concrete experience (Sense)

We are constantly experiencing a multitude of sensory information from the outside world. That information is directed to the area of the brain that deals with sensory information. Zull refers to this as the sensory cortex, a term used to group various regions of the cerebral cortex that deal with touch, taste, vision, sound and smell. This variety of sensory input represents your concrete experience.

Reflective observation (Integrate)

Reflection happens in the temporal integrative cortex. Our reflective skills allow us to integrate the concrete experience we have received via our senses into something tangible that has meaning.

Long-term explicit memories are formed in this region, in which the hippocampus plays a major role. The left hemisphere allows us to comprehend the detail of language and the right hemisphere the meaning with regard to how things are being said, intonation and intention. We will find ourselves drifting off in a daydream state, finding connections to related images.

This reflective process may respond with images and memories similar to the new incoming information. When we read that there are 100 billion brain cells in the brain, while reflecting on this we remember there are 100 billion trees in the rainforest; suddenly we see a picture of huge rainforest trees, with dendritic branches and cell bodies in the centre, with the trunk appearing like an axon carrying signals to other trees from miles around, the rainforest alive with electrical and chemical activity. In an instant it can throw back this type of imagery and give meaning to something that was new to us. We now have an understanding of the scale of the neuronal networks in our brain.

Abstract hypothesis (Integrate)
Our front integrative cortex allows us to build on what we know, create new connections, explore possibilities, judge whether it makes sense based on what we know, use our working memory to manipulate the information, question our back integrative cortex for more information and bring all this back and make evaluations based on our experience.

If the concrete information has not made any sense to us, it can work with the back integrative cortex, questioning for possible meaning. It can create new images and 'what if' scenarios, effectively helping to construct possible new memories.

In short, it is the director of your brain, allowing us to take ownership of the information, make decisions about it and prime us for action: the Steven Spielberg of your mind – creating, editing, questioning and producing something that can be acted upon.

Active testing (Act)
If the front integrative cortex is the director, the pre-motor and motor cortex are the actors, taking action in the form of voluntary movement and speech. Testing out ideas in order to receive more sensory information. This action may come in the form of speaking, rehearsing, building, writing or moving.

Action – Using the learning cycle

Time limit: 5 minutes
- ▶ Sensory input: How would you use this model to help remember that the capital city of Madagascar is Antananarivo?
- ▶ Reflection: What memories, images and understandings do you have about Madagascar and Antananarivo? What comes to mind?
- ▶ Abstraction: How might you make this information more memorable? What do you need to know?
- ▶ Action: Find out what you need to know. Draw a picture to represent the information, write the words or make them out of clay and say them aloud. Explain how you did this to a friend; ask how they might do it.

It is likely that you will jump around and do some of these things out of sequence, perhaps run the cycle a number of times.

Insight

When I first started using memory techniques back in the early 1990s, it seemed clear to me that to truly understand, you have to experience, and to remember that experience, it has to have meaning and a purpose for you. If you are a programmer, there is no use in just understanding syntax, you need to physically build applications to fully appreciate the craftsmanship involved. If you learn a language, you have to go and put it into practice for it to become implicitly useful. As the saying goes, 'If you don't use it, you lose it.' As clichéd as this is, it stands true, even more so when we understand that our brain's neuronal networks get stronger the more they fire off and, if they stop firing, those connections can stop working.

Emotion and motivation

Joining the learning cycle together is emotion, the area in the limbic cortex that lets us experience pain and pleasure. Emotions are our motivators. They can prime us and direct our attention; they can intensify our memories and add meaning to them.

You instinctively know that if you are interested in something, you are more likely to remember it; likewise if you are afraid of something or you know that something will be a painful experience, you will definitely remember this in order to avoid it.

You could use this knowledge to prime yourself for key information within a book, presentation or seminar. Your reticular activation system (reticular formation), located within your brain stem, is permanently turned on – it directs your attention to anything that is of importance to you. You may have had the experience when you have bought a new computer. You loved it, it gave you loads of pleasure, until now you haven't noticed anyone with one, you thought you were the first to get one – but now suddenly 'everyone' has one. Your senses have been primed!

Priming your senses

Action – Priming your senses

Time limit: 3 minutes
- Take a moment to look around the room.
- Try to remember everything you see that is GREEN.
- Now keep staring at this book – DO NOT LOOK AWAY!
- With your EYES CLOSED say out loud everything in the room that is blue.
- What have you learned from this?

Framing your learning

The learning cycle is a great way of 'framing' how we think about learning that creates understanding and is memorable. It makes sure that when working with new information, you touch on every stage.

In the upcoming chapters we will build on the knowledge of our model of how memory works and the learning cycle and show how you can utilize specific techniques and a way of thinking that will rapidly increase your effectiveness in how to remember and deliver value from your actions.

We will be exploring how you can become more receptive to sensory information. How can you create the optimum environment both externally and internally for the sensory information you receive? You will learn techniques to improve reflection and abstraction that will help with memory and understanding, all with a view to what action can be taken.

You might want to think of the rest of this book as 'living' the learning cycle. As you are exposed to some new ideas or information, be encouraged to reflect on your own experiences, explore and take ownership of where this fits in with your own life, become an active participant by putting what you learn into practice.

KEYS TO A GREAT MEMORY

▶ Use the basis of the learning cycle, Sense → Integrate → Act to frame all your learning.

▶ You have a concrete experience through a multitude of sensory inputs.

▶ Reflective observation relates sensory input to things you already know in a search for understanding and meaning.

▶ Use abstract hypothesis to deeply integrate new information through questioning and exploring possibilities.

▶ Put what you have learned into practice through active testing and receive feedback in the form of more sensory input allowing you to learn and grow.

▶ Emotion is the motivator: get curious and look for how new information will help you achieve your purpose and give you pleasure and avoid pain.

▶ Prime yourself before reading a book or listening to a presentation by thinking about what might be important to you.

▶ Become an active participant in your learning; use everything you learn in some way.

Part 2
A new way of thinking

'Imagination is everything. It is the preview of life's coming attractions.'

Albert Einstein

3

··

Creative memorization: Unleash your true memory potential

In this chapter you will learn:
- *the process for creative memorization*
- *how to develop the four core skills*
- *how to make information more memorable*
- *how to put creative memorization into practice.*

Memory and creativity

At the heart of memorization are sets of skills that allow us to remember vast amounts of information, store it in long-term memory and recall it at any time with minimal revision. You can think of this set of skills as creative memorization. Once mastered, it is possible to memorize an entire book, remember the names of 50 people in a room or details of an hour-long presentation. At the heart of creative memorization are four core skills:

- ▶ **Relaxation** – the ability to release tension from your body
- ▶ **Concentration** – to enter into a focused state of mind (trance state), free from inhibitions
- ▶ **Imagination** – to create memorable experiences using senses and emotion
- ▶ **Association** – to find creative ways of connecting, questioning and analysing.

The good news is you already possess the skills you need to memorize anything you put your mind to; in fact, as a child you probably spent most of your time strengthening them. However, through lack of use some may have diminished over time. With creative memorization the difference between a person's ability to remember or forget is all about approach and the intensity with which these skills are applied.

Insight

In practice you want to remember that Burkina Faso's capital is Ouagadougou. Using creative memorization you see a BARKING dog with a mean FACE (Barkin' Face, Burkina Faso) but he is a good WAGGY DOGGY (Waggy Doggy, Ouagadougou). By repeating the 'real words' aloud and 'seeing' the image simultaneously, you create a strong connection between the image and the information. You now know that Ouagadougou is the capital of Burkina Faso.

Action – Benchmark your core skills

Time limit: 5 minutes
Take a moment to write down the answers to the following questions:

▶ What are the things you currently do to relax and release tension?

▶ How do you achieve a concentrated and focused state of mind?

▶ Think of a time when you had to be imaginative. Where were you, what were you doing, what challenges did you have and what was the outcome?

▶ How good are you at making connections, solving problems and identifying patterns? When have you done this and what were the results?

▶ On a scale of 1–10 (10 being excellent), how good would you say you were at each one of these core skills?

▶ On a piece of A4 paper write down each of the four core skills or draw a picture which represents them. Next to each one write down the number you gave for the level you are currently at. Stick this up where it will be visible. We will use this to measure your improvement over the course of the book.

Memory techniques have been around for over 2,000 years and have been reinvented many times. The essence of creative memorization is the ability to use our imagination and association to construct vivid memories that can be stored and easily recalled.

Action – Test your association skills

Time limit: 5 minutes

Read the following ten words and say aloud the first word you associate with each one, then write it down. It is important not to 'think' too hard or edit what is in your mind even if you think it is ridiculous – for Ricky Gervais you might say 'funny', 'loud' or 'the office'. The associations you come up with will be personal to you.

- ▶ Ricky Gervais
- ▶ Dumbo
- ▶ Chaplin
- ▶ Nemo
- ▶ Ugly
- ▶ Fight
- ▶ Caboose
- ▶ French
- ▶ Smoke
- ▶ Karova

For every word in this list (whether you are aware of it or not) you will have an image sparked off by an association you have with it. In some cases, as with Nemo, it may be because you have watched the film *Finding Nemo*, so you say the word 'fish', this is a natural association. With a word like *karova*, unless you know that it is Russian for 'cow', your image may have been 'a car' because the first part of the word sounds like 'car ', 'Car – rova' or a bottle of 'Corona'. Even though you don't know what it means, your brain will go searching for a connection and bring something back. Perhaps you read one of these words and simply told yourself that you didn't know what it means, in which case you may have had a brief image of the word itself and then your brain ceased looking for an association.

Insight

Your brain will pay close attention to what you say. Have you ever had the experience of meeting someone who you haven't seen for a long time, you recognize their face, know that you knew them, perhaps even really well, but you just can't remember the name, then a couple of days or weeks later their name pops into your mind? The reason behind this is that you asked a question with the expectation of getting an answer and so your brain goes off in search of one. If, on the other hand, you told yourself 'I can't remember' or 'I don't know it', your brain will stop looking for those connections.

The creative state of mind

Konstantin Stanislavsky, renowned for the Stanislavsky acting technique, referred to the creative state of mind as 'the artistic condition that frees the body of tension and energizes the creative faculties' (from Mel Gordon's *The Stanislavsky Technique*).

THE STANISLAVSKY TECHNIQUE

The Stanislavsky technique contains a set of exercises to improve relaxation, concentration and imagination, which culminate in the ability to enter into what Stanislavsky referred to as the 'creative state of mind'. In Mel Gordon's workbook for actors, *The Stanislavsky Technique*, he pulls together techniques used throughout Stanislavsky's life.

Konstantin Stanislavsky

In 1912 Konstantin Stanislavsky (originally, Konstantin Sergeyevich Alexeyev) opened the Moscow Art Theatre's first studio, condensing years of work into a set of specific techniques, known as the Stanislavsky techniques. Two of his greatest students, YevgenyVakhtangov and Michael Chekhov, went on to create variations of his work, influencing actors around the globe for years to come. In the USA, Lee Strasberg created 'The Method', a system derived from Stanislavsky's techniques which is now mostly known through actors such as Dustin Hoffman, Robert De Niro, Marilyn Monroe, James Dean and Paul Newman to name but a few.

There are and always have been differences of opinion as to the value of Stanislavsky's techniques to innately talented actors. An example of this might be the infamous conversation between Dustin Hoffman (a 'method' actor) and Laurence Olivier on the set of the film *Marathon Man* (1976), where Hoffman had apparently been running around the block in preparation for a scene in which he was out of breath. When Olivier, bemused by this behaviour, asked what he was doing, Hoffman questioned how else could he prepare for the scene. To which Olivier retorted, 'Try acting, dear boy.' Whether this is true or not, in acting circles it is a story which is retold when debate breaks out about the Stanislavsky technique or 'The Method'.

Many of these techniques provide a useful framework when it comes to improving the core skills required in creative memorization.

Insight
The techniques laid down by Stanislavsky provide numerous ways in which to enter the creative state of mind. However you access it, this state is exactly the place you need to be when you wish to comprehend, store, retain and recall information. It is no coincidence that the majority of competent actors have the ability to memorize numerous plays word for word and recite monologues from them years later. Although actors may not be aware of it, they are using very similar creative memorization skills employed by memory champions to remember over 2,000 digits in an hour. Other techniques from Stanislavsky to do with objectives, actions, justification and units provide an excellent framework when memorizing more advanced information such as books, law, speeches and presentations.

Core skills

RELAXATION

There are many ways of achieving states of relaxation: regular meditation or exercises such as tai chi, yoga, qigong and pilates are excellent in releasing tension, energizing and creating an awareness of your body. For creative memorization the ideal state is to be relaxed, energized and free from tension.

Action – Achieve energy and relaxation

Time limit: 10 minutes
- Try this deep diaphragmatic breathing exercise that will relax, focus and energize your body. Breathe at this ratio – in for 1 hold for 4 out for 2 – so you may breathe in for 8, hold for 32 out for 16. Repeat this 10 times. Practise this three times a day to relax and increase energy (from *Personal Power*, Tony Robbins).
- Sit on a chair, get yourself into a comfortable position and just be aware of your body pressing against the chair. While breathing deeply pay attention to each part of your body in turn, starting with your feet and working through your knees, thighs, all the way up to the top of your head. As you work your way up, notice how much tension there is. Each time you notice some tension, take a breath and breathe out to release it.

- Clench the fist of your right hand, breathe in and as you breathe out let go of all tension. Repeat this with your left fist, then feel the tension releasing from your entire body.
- Pick up an object and notice how much energy is needed. Put it down. Try it again and this time use the least amount of energy possible, become aware of which muscles are engaging, put the object down and release all tension from your muscles. Repeat this exercise with different objects (from *The Stanislavsky Technique*, Mel Gordon).

CONCENTRATION

Relaxation and concentration are closely connected. Together they create a state of focus ideal for memorization. With practice you can train yourself to a level where you can block out all distractions.

Action – Concentration and focus

Time limit: 10 minutes

- Focus on a spot on the wall while picking up the sounds of everything around you. While focusing on this spot, identify each sound before moving on to the next one. See how many sounds you can identify and try to judge where they are coming from.
- Turn on the TV, then the radio, and at the same time have someone try to engage you in conversation while you perform a task that requires concentration. This might be reading a book, writing some emails or solving a problem.
- Begin several activities: look at magazine pictures, listen to music, solve a mathematical problem, play a game, check your email, make a phone call. Move quickly from one activity to another. In each activity, concentrate completely on the first before you pass on to the next (from *The Stanislavsky Technique*, Mel Gordon).
- Close your eyes and mentally transport yourself to a location of your choice. Walk around that location paying close attention to objects (from *The Stanislavsky Technique*, Mel Gordon).

IMAGINATION

Imagination is the foundation of creative memorization. The ability not just to create vivid images using all of our five senses but to suspend belief about what is and isn't possible, take ourselves into a world of fantasy, excite our curiosity and recapture those childlike moments of inspiration.

By strengthening this skill, it is possible to intensify the memories we create, bring them alive, exaggerate them, give them rhythm and movement and make them instantly memorable, transferring them into long-term memory.

Action – Engaging your imagination

Time limit: 10 minutes

▶ Focus on a simple object, study it, then recreate it in your mind in every detail. Engage each of your five senses.

▶ Focus on a different object; imagine it sprouting arms, legs and a face. Ask what it wants and listen to what it says. Now close your eyes and recreate the object, notice where you visualize the object in your mind, have a conversation with the object. Try switching between eyes closed and eyes open.

▶ Imagine a flower growing from a seed in the ground into a full plant. Closing your eyes, follow the process of its growth and development (from *The Stanislavsky Technique*, Mel Gordon).

▶ Remember a street or path that you walk past daily. Break it into separate sections. Create a story that links each of the sections of the street (from *The Stanislavsky Technique*, Mel Gordon).

▶ Find resemblances between objects and specific persons. Find resemblances between selected persons and animals. Study them in your mind (from *The Stanislavsky Technique*, Mel Gordon).

Affective memory

A key skill in the Stanislavsky technique was the ability to recreate feelings and emotions; while this is obviously useful for an actor, it is also a skill that can greatly intensify a memory. Stanislavsky referred to this as 'affective memory' and it can be broken down into two parts: sense memory, which allows you to create sensations, and emotional recall, which allows you to create emotion.

Insight

In creative memorization the skill of not just seeing the image in your mind but feeling, tasting, hearing and smelling it, as well as incorporating emotions such as joy, humour, tragedy, fear or arousal, allows you to go much further than simply turning information into pictures: it translates potentially dry or complex information into memorable experiences.

Action – Develop your sense memory (creating concrete experience)

Time limit: 10 minutes

▶ Make a cup of tea, paying close attention to every movement and sense. As you drink it, notice the various sensations in your body. Now create another cup of tea using only your imagination, recreate every feeling in detail – pay attention to all five senses.

▶ Imagine you are waiting for a bus in the rain, you don't have a jacket and it's cold. Close your eyes and recreate what it feels like – make it real and engage each one of your senses. Now imagine someone else is at the bus stop: how do they feel?

▶ Light a match. Repeat the activity until you strongly feel every detail of it. Now perform the activity again without the actual matches (from *The Stanislavsky Technique*, Mel Gordon).

▶ Complete the following activities without any real objects: wash your hair, put clothes on, shave, sew with a needle, sharpen a pencil, now sharpen a pencil with a knife. Create a complete and convincing action without worrying about the miming of each activity (from *The Stanislavsky Technique*, Mel Gordon).

Action – Develop your emotional recall

Time limit: 10 minutes

▶ Remember all the foods you ate as a child. Describe their flavours and textures. Experience the taste of them and how you felt (from *The Stanislavsky Technique*, Mel Gordon).

▶ Remember the house or flat where you grew up. Describe it. Imagine you are there now and notice the emotions you feel (from *The Stanislavsky Technique*, Mel Gordon).

- Think back to the first day of school. Now focus on an object, maybe your school bag, notice the smell and how heavy it is. Remember a situation from one of those early days and experience the emotions you had.
- Imagine it is late at night and you are sitting on the sofa when you hear a bang in another room. Experience how that feels. Imagine you can hear creaking floorboards and then the light switches off. Take a moment to analyse the intensity of the emotions you experienced.
- Imagine it's late at night and there is a knock on the door. As you walk to the door you can hear the familiar voices of your friends, you open the door and see two of your friends being held by four large men with balaclavas. Again take a moment to notice the intensity of your sensations.

Choose one sense memory exercise and one emotional recall exercise and this time gauge where you are on a scale of 1–10.

- Practise minimizing and magnifying your senses and emotions along that scale.
- Notice the differences and see how quickly you can change levels of feeling and emotion.

ASSOCIATION

When we think of a past event, we are reminded of details associated with it. We remember Christmas, birthdays and holidays because they have strong associations, they are emotional and have excited our senses.

The events that happen to us affect how we feel, how we act and what we remember. Association is a very powerful tool when it comes to memorizing information. If imagination is the foundation of creative memorization, association is the glue that binds those memories together – imagination and association are intrinsically linked. Throughout our lives we are constantly creating associations; memories, beliefs or feelings we have towards people and things are all formed through various types of associations. The more intense the association, the more memorable it becomes as our neurons form strong synaptic connections.

Association focuses on key left-brain activities such as questioning, analytical thinking and recognizing patterns. In creative memorization this translates into looking for the best way to encode information into images and connect them in a manner that is memorable.

Natural-image and sound-image associations
When it comes to thinking up an image to represent a word or piece of information, there is not always an instant association or at least not one that feels very clear. When there is not a natural association, you will need to create an image that sounds similar to all or part of the keyword; this is known as a sound-image association and is a vital skill to develop if you want to progress to advanced levels of creative memorization.

There are two methods for doing this that with practice become second nature. With both methods the meaning of the word can play an essential part in creating an image for your information.

▶ Natural-image associations – images sparked off by a memory, sense or emotion.
▶ Sound-image associations – images that sound very similar to the information you are memorizing.

NATURAL-IMAGE ASSOCIATION
These are all very personal, so I will give you examples of how these words relate to myself; chances are they will have a very different meaning for you.

▶ Awesome – the first image that comes to mind for me is an awesome tidal wave. So I would use tidal wave as my image.
▶ Fearless – a fearless lion or someone you know who was fearless in the past.
▶ Scary – Freddy Kruger, or a similar kind of scary image.

SOUND-IMAGE ASSOCIATION
▶ Madagascar – if you have been here, then you may have an emotional association. If not, we need to look at how the word sounds: a mad – gas – car could represent Madagascar.
▶ Capitulate – the first part of the word is cap, so your image could be a cap. The meaning of capitulate is to surrender or give up. So you could imagine a cap kneeling down with his hands clasped together, surrendering, giving up. This way you remember the word and also what it means.

- Accentuate – the first part of this word sounds like axe, so your image could be an axe. Accentuate means to emphasize, highlight, make more noticeable. So you could imagine your axe in a spotlight, emphasizing its tap dancing skills.

As you can probably see, this is also a great way to expand your vocabulary.

Recite the information
An important point to note is that when you look at your mental image you should speak the word out loud; the more obscure the word, the more important this is. By doing this you are creating more mental connections with the image and the sound of the word and helping to lock it in your mind. Within the context of the learning cycle, you are actively testing.

Obviously memorizing like this will seem strange at first, but then again, what new thing we learn doesn't? As I said before, practise something enough and it will eventually become second nature; when it's second nature, it feels the natural thing to do.

Action – Natural-image and sound-image association

Time limit: 5 minutes
The easiest way to develop this skill is to practise turning random words into images. The sound-image is a trigger for the real word. Here is an example of how you could use both sound-images and natural associations to make words more memorable. While imagining the following you should be in a relaxed, focused state and engage all of your five senses. It is essential to say the word aloud while visualizing it in your mind:

- Chore – you're dressed like Cinderella doing a chore – say 'chore' aloud (natural)
- Astride – you are astride a horse – say 'astride' aloud (natural)
- Subscript – there is a SUBmarine reading a SCRIPT – say 'subscript' aloud (sound)
- Misjudge – a MISS JUDGE (sound)

- ▶ Purified – a purifying filtration unit (natural)
- ▶ Braised – a braised bit of beef (natural)
- ▶ Semblance – SAME BLINDS (sound)
- ▶ Covertly – special ops under a COVER (natural/sound)
- ▶ Bravo – clapping, shouting 'Bravo!' (natural)
- ▶ Mantel – hanging off the mantel (natural)
- ▶ August – Roman Emperor (natural)

The power of questions

Questions are the guiding force for your associations so it is important to ask the right questions in order to receive a good answer. You should also create a feeling of expectation while asking the question. If you expect to get an answer, at some point you will receive feedback. It may not always be the answer you are looking for, but you will get a response. The power of asking questions is essential in your ability not only to create associations but also to recall them.

Action – What are your key questions?

Time limit: 5 minutes
Reflect on some of the questions below and ask yourself which ones would be useful to you with regard to creative memorization:

- ▶ How can I do this?
- ▶ What would happen if?
- ▶ What am I missing?
- ▶ What's the best way to connect this?
- ▶ How can I make this funnier, scarier or sexy?
- ▶ How can I intensify this?
- ▶ What happens next?
- ▶ What shouldn't happen next?
- ▶ If I were that object/image, what would I do?
- ▶ Where is the best place for this?

Choose or create five key questions you will ask when using creative memorization.

In practice

Creative memorization is exactly what it says: the process of using your creativity to make information more memorable. The pair game is a simple game that allows you to unite the core skills within creative memorization – Relaxation, Concentration, Imagination and Association. The objective of the game is to memorize as many pairs of words as possible.

Action – The pair game

Time limit: 5 minutes

▶ Use the relaxation and concentration technique of your choice; with practice you will be able to go into this focused state almost instantaneously.

▶ Look at the first pair of words and let an image for each word come into your mind – go for the first natural image that appears. If it doesn't appear straight away, use your questioning skills to figure out what would be a good sound-image.

▶ Once you have an image for each word, associate them together – for Krypton + Plug, you may imagine Superman wearing a plug made of kryptonite trying to throw it off before he collapses.

▶ Use your imagination to intensify the images and engage senses. You may imagine that you are Superman and physically act out the scene.

▶ Finally, repeat the words aloud 3–5 times while focusing on the image – this is essential to associate the words to the image.

Give yourself five minutes to play this game. At the end you will be tested to see how many pairs of words you remember by seeing one of the words and responding with its corresponding pair, e.g. What is the pair word for 'plug'?

krypton + plug

pyramid + camera

laptop + ribbon

speaker + frustration

phone + sing

pencil + trumpet

cola + fast

establish + no

lightning + green

soft + consult

friend + armour

weights + sea

gift + product

radio + Chris

section + blow

Write down the correct word next to its pair:

consult

camera

laptop

section

sing

pencil

cola

krypton

no

lightning

Chris

armour

sea

gift

frustration

The concepts and ideas behind creative memorization are fairly simple; mastering them, however, takes dedication. By immersing yourself in these techniques, the benefits and rewards will become clear as you start to apply them in your everyday life.

KEYS TO A GREAT MEMORY

▶ Creative memorization is the ability to use imagination and association in order to make sensory information more memorable.

▶ Make a note of the level at which you benchmarked your skills so you can compare the results at the end of the book.

▶ Practise some simple relaxation techniques you can use before learning so your body is free from tension; consider an activity such as qigong, tai chi or yoga.

▶ Practise trying to remember something while being distracted, to improve your focus.

▶ Notice everyday objects and recreate them in your mind, involving all of your five senses to strengthen your imagination.

▶ Act out day-to-day activities such as making the tea to develop your sense memory.

▶ Practise remembering events and situations and recall the emotion to intensify the memory.

▶ While practising sense memory and emotional recall, play with the levels of intensity by imagining magnifying the feelings on a scale from 1–10.

▶ Play with turning words into natural-images and sound-images to build your creative memorization skills.

▶ Use the power of questions to guide 'how' you associate information and make it memorable.

4

Reference stories: Making information memorable

In this chapter you will learn:
- *how to create a reference story*
- *being 'selective' when encoding or decoding information*
- *dialling up your stories to make them stick*
- *how to use active daydreaming when you get stumped.*

When applying the process of creative memorization, you are effectively encoding, storing and retrieving (decoding) reference stories. Each reference story will act as a 'reference' to the actual information that will presumably benefit you in some way. You may think of a reference story as a container that holds a set of natural-images and/or sound-images: the meaning of these images refers to some real-world information. Therefore a reference story is the tangible artefact you produce when using creative memorization.

When creating reference stories, you have the option to use visual embedding or narratives. The narratives may have context and feel like a micro-story while visual embedding uses a repetitive pattern for associations. The latter is often used by memory athletes to quickly store numbers in competition by visually embedding images from left to right or top to bottom along a pre-ordained journey.

Encoding

Encoding is the process of converting your information into reference stories. Here are the steps you go through when encoding information using creative memorization:

- ▶ Identify the information you wish to remember.
- ▶ Reflect on your natural-images and/or sound-images.
- ▶ Abstract and create your reference story using either a narrative or visual embedding.
- ▶ Actively test your story by reciting aloud, writing it down or using it in some way – *important: you must mentally see the images as you say the 'real' information.*

Decoding

Decoding is the ability to deconstruct a reference story and convert it back into the information. The following is an example of the steps you go through to decode a reference story:

- ▶ You may be asked a question or try to recall the information.
- ▶ This will trigger the memory of the reference story.
- ▶ Decode the reference story into its component parts and understand its meaning.
- ▶ With repetition you will eventually bypass the reference story and just 'know' the information.

VISUAL EMBEDDING

Visual embedding is a simple and consistent approach that you can use when memorizing small chunks of information. You follow the same pattern of connecting images each time, usually from left to right or top to bottom.

Action – How to use visual embedding

Time limit: 5 minutes
- ▶ Take your main item (in this case the cow).
- ▶ You can embed up to three bits of information on to the cow (these items should be smaller).
- ▶ The positions you can embed go from top to bottom (head, middle, feet).
- ▶ While embedding, use sense memory to experience the connections.

- ▶ After embedding zoom back and see the big picture.
- ▶ As you look at the image say [image] – [meaning]: [cow] – [karova].
- ▶ Repeat 5–20 times at speed.

Figure 4.1 Encoding (1).

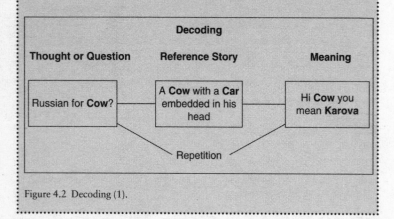

Figure 4.2 Decoding (1).

NARRATIVES

Narratives form a micro-story to connect information together in a sequence; they don't necessarily form any consistent pattern and can therefore be different every time. They often play with the context of the information being memorized. A Cow looking up at the sky sees a Car jumping over the moon. Taking something previously related to the word and changing the context.

Action – How to use narratives

Time limit: 5 minutes
Utilizing imagination in your narratives

- ▶ Always engage your senses
- ▶ Exaggerate your images in some way
- ▶ Bring them to life (involve your emotions)

Optional

- ▶ Put yourself in the story or imagine you are characters in the story
- ▶ Imagine your images in front of you

Associations

- ▶ Don't over analyse your associations – anything is possible
- ▶ Focus on connecting 2–3 items together at a time
- ▶ Connect using a narrative or simply stick one item into the other
- ▶ Use movement and action to create 'a flow'

Optional

- ▶ Act out! If you are in the story while you see the images in front of you, this is a form of actively testing your story.

Figure 4.3 Encoding (2).

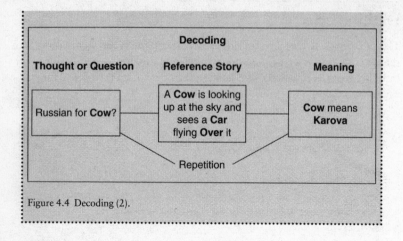

Figure 4.4 Decoding (2).

SELECTIVE MEMORY AND MINIMAL IMAGES NECESSARY (MIN)

In order for creative memorization to help us in our everyday life or progress our career, it is important to be selective about the information we encode by making sure that it is valuable to us in some way. There can be the temptation to create images for everything; however, this will most likely lead to a sense of frustration. It is therefore not only important but also advantageous to only encode the minimal number of images necessary to spark off the key information at a later date.

In simple terms – if you already know it, then there's probably no need to encode. If one image can trigger off everything you need to know, then that's enough. Your goal should be to use the minimum number of images necessary in order to remember the key information and take some form of valuable action.

Insight

One of the most common questions I have experienced across my career is, 'Isn't it easier just to remember the information rather than creating stories to represent them?' The answer to this will be different for every individual. If you find that you can remember text from books, facts, numbers, names, etc. without the need for any type of creative memorization, then that's what you should do. For most people this isn't the case and there will be specific areas where they need help or can improve. A good question to ask is 'What don't I know and how could creative memorization help?'

Dialling up

This is a simple technique you can use to dial up the intensity of your reference stories, making them bigger, brighter and more memorable. Initially, you can practise this with simple imagery and then move on to more complex reference stories.

Action – Dial up the apple

Time limit: 10 minutes
Imagine you have a dial with the numbers 1–10 either in front of you or on your wrist. Take a moment and imagine this dial in every detail:

- ▶ What is the shape of the face of the dial?
- ▶ What does the pointer of the dial look like?
- ▶ What is it made of?
- ▶ What colour is it?
- ▶ How does it feel?
- ▶ How big is it?
- ▶ Is it hot or cold?
- ▶ Does it get hotter the more you turn it up?
- ▶ Play with the dial, moving it up and down through the numbers 1–10.
- ▶ Do the numbers change colour as you do this?
- ▶ Do the numbers get bigger or smaller as you move up and down?
- ▶ Close your eyes and spend a few minutes seeing this dial in every detail, make it your dial, something you can use at any time to increase the intensity of the memories that you create.
- ▶ Now let us use the dial to intensify a simple image. Imagine that in front of you is an apple, just an ordinary apple. As you look at this apple you can see the dial moving on its own; if the image of the apple, is not very clear, it will be drawn towards the 1, if it is bright and vibrant, if you can taste and feel it, if it is big and solid it will move towards the 10.
- ▶ As you look at the apple you watch where the dial rests, take control of the dial and very slowly move the dial all the way down. Notice what happens as you do this: does it become

less clear? Do the colours drift away; perhaps it becomes black and white? Does it become more transparent or completely disappear? Take a moment and in your own time take control of the dial and move it slowly down to 1.

▶ Now in your own time, very slowly start to dial up the intensity of the apple, moving up through the numbers. Notice how the apple changes, notice how it grows bigger and brighter, more colourful and vibrant as you move up on your way to the higher numbers. Notice how real it becomes, until it's larger than life. Perhaps it actually comes to life? What happens as you move up to the number 10? Spend a moment and enjoy the intensity of the memory you are creating.

▶ Finally, spend a few minutes moving the dial up and down. As you take complete control of your dial, notice how you can make the apple completely disappear or burst into life right in front of you.

Try using your dial with some of the reference stories you created for the countries and capitals. Run through the story in your mind and notice where the dial is. When you are ready, take control of the dial and move it up through the numbers – if it's on a 3, just move it to 5 initially and notice the difference in how clear the story seems. Then move it to 7, then 9, then 10. Run the story forwards and backwards a few times with the dial at a high number.

Insight

Dialling up can be a very powerful tool. I tend to use it with information I wish to remember for long periods of time, or presentations which need to be locked in my mind and roll off the tongue. My suggestion would be to keep it simple in the beginning; when practising some of the sense memory exercises, see what happens when you dial them up.

Active daydreaming

Daydreaming can have a lot of negative associations: most people at some point in their lives have been told to 'stop daydreaming'. Perhaps people often referred to you as 'a daydreamer'. This usually implies that you have a lack of concentration and can't focus on what is 'really important'.

Daydreaming can be a very powerful skill. In essence, daydreaming is the ability to go into a trance state. You may have experienced this when driving your car and ending up at your destination not quite remembering the last five minutes, or sitting in a meeting room only to find that you've lost the thread of the conversation. More than likely it can happen when presentations are happening, and you find yourself doodling and going off on a journey in your mind.

You can think of active daydreaming as the ability to lightly direct and guide your thoughts to produce positive results. It is the point where you become less aware of your conscious thoughts and have the ability to access your unconscious resources.

Insight

As a hypnotherapist, I find it useful when guiding a person into trance to compare it to this daydreaming state as it is something that everyone has experienced and creates a clear point of reference as to what to expect when you are hypnotized. I personally find it useful to think of entering into this state when creating ideas, solving problems or creating reference stories.

Action – How many uses for a safety pin?

Time limit: 3 minutes
How many uses could there be for a safety pin? If there were no limits and the laws of physics didn't exist? Let yourself actively daydream on this thought after you've read through the process below.

▶ Ask yourself a question that guides you towards an outcome, i.e. What can I currently use a safety pin for? What can't I use a safety pin for? (If you can't use it to fly a plane, imagine how you might construct a network of safety pins that form the wheel and control panels.)
▶ 'Anything is possible', there is no 'cannot'.
▶ 'Expect' to get answers to your questions.
▶ Get yourself into a relaxed state of mind.
▶ Let your thoughts drift.
▶ As imagery and ideas pop into your mind, capture them in some way (mind maps and visual thinking are ideal for this – or just write the words, doodle and draw pictures).
▶ Continue to gently ask questions and let your mind drift. When your mind goes off at a tangent, enjoy the experience and know that your brain is searching for connections.

In practice

Action – The capitals game

Time limit: 30 minutes
Use the time to create reference stories for the following 17
countries and capitals. This game pushes you to encode the
information and produce reference stories as quickly as you can.
You should aim to go faster than feels comfortable; if you get
stuck, move on. There are examples you can use, although it will
work better if you use your own.

▶ The first country is Burundi and its capital is Bujumbura. First
  create images to represent the information – these images do
  not have to be complex; they just have to be something that
  sparks off enough of the word to help you remember.
▶ Burundi sounds like Brandy (B ran dy): we will use this as our
  sound-image[s].
▶ Bujumbura sounds like BeeJambra (Bee Jam Bra): this is
  another sound-image[s].
▶ Now we create a reference story – imagine a large glass of
  Brandy is being drunk by a Bee covered in sticky Jam and
  wearing a pink Bra OR large glass of Brandy, Bee embedded
  on top, Jam in sides, Bra in middle.
▶ It is important to make this reference story feel real. Think
  of everything you have learned from creative memorization:
  engage all of your senses, exaggerate the size of the images,
  imagine this happening right in front of you, perhaps 'you' are
  the bee – play around and see what feels good. Abstract your
  own ideas, own the experience.
▶ As you imagine this reference story, actively test it – see the
  Brandy, then say the word Burundi, this will 'connect' the
  sound-image to the real word and will help consolidate the
  'meaning'. Next see the Bee Jam bra and repeat the capital
  Bujumbura out loud. Make a physical action as you repeat the
  information and say the image.
▶ Repeat this process at least five times.
▶ Now see the reference story in reverse and say the capital first
  and which country it belongs to. By doing this you are creating
  more connections with the information.
▶ Finally, write down the country and its capital.

Sensory information Country – Capital	Integrate images [n]/[s]	Integrate reference story	Active testing
Burundi – Bujumbura	Brandy[s] – BeeJamBra[s]	a large glass of **Brandy** is being drunk by a **Bee** covered in sticky **Jam** and wearing a pink **Bra**	Burundi's capital is Bujumbura
Comoros – Moroni	Cameras[s] – Moron[s]	lots of **Cameras** being used by a **Moron**	Comoros's capital is Moroni
Djibouti – Djibouti	JBoot[s]	2 **Boots** that are in the shape of a **J**	Djibouti's capital is Djibouti
Eritrea – Asmara	AirTree[s] – Asthma[s]	a tree is trying to get some air **AirTree** as it is suffering from **Asthma**	Eritrea's capital is Asmara
Ethiopia – Addis Ababa	Ethiopia[n] – AdidasBaby[n]	an Adidas Baby in Ethiopia	Ethiopia's capital is Addis Ababa
Kenya – Nairobi	Can[s] – NoRobe[s]	a **Can** covering up someone you know with **No Robes**	Kenya's capital is Nairobi
Madagascar – Antananarivo	Lion (Alex)[n] – Antenna[s]	**Alex the Lion** from Madagascar is wearing an **Antenna** on his head	Madagascar's capital in Antananarivo
Malawi – Lilongwe	MaleLawWee[s] – LongWee[s]	a **Male** who is involved in **Law** having a **Long Wee**	Malawi's capital is Lilongwe
Mauritania – Nouakchott	MoriartyTan[s] – KnockShot[s]	Moriarty has a Tan and Knocks before taking a Shot at Holmes	Mauritania's capital is Nouakchott

(*continued*)

Sensory information Country – Capital	Integrate images [n]/[s]	Integrate reference story	Active testing
Mozambique – Maputo	MossBeak[s] – MyPutter[s]	a bird with a **MossBeak** is eating **MyPutter**	Mozambique's capital is Maputo
Rwanda – Kigali	Rwand[s] – Giggly[s]	a wizard is holding an **R wand** and is very **Giggly**	Rwanda's capital is Kigali
Seychelles – Victoria	SeaShells[s] – Victoria[n]	**SeaShells** are being made into a statue of **Queen Victoria**	Seychelles's capital is Victoria
Somalia – Mogadishu	Semolina[s] – MuckyDish[s]	left over **Semolina** has made a **MuckyDish**	Somalia's capital is Mogadishu
Tanzania – Dar-es-Salaam	Tasmanian devil[n] – DoorsSlam[s]	**Tasmanian devil** in a hall full of **Doors Slamming** them	Tanzania's capital is Dar-es-Salaam
Uganda – Kampala	UGun[s] – CampPole[s]	a **UGun** (gun in the shape of a U) blasts a **CampPole**	Uganda's capital is Kampala
Zambia – Lusaka	ZoomBeer[s] – LooSack[s]	a **Zoom**ing **Beer** falls into a **LooSack**	Zambia's capital is Lusaka
Zimbabwe – Harare	ZoomBaby[s] – Hairy[s]	a **Zoom**ing **Baby** is very **Hairy**	Zimbabwe's capital is Harare

Insight

It has been my experience that when a person starts using creative memorization and creating reference stories, at first it can feel like a real challenge. This is why I have found it extremely beneficial with the people I have worked with to give them lots of examples to get them started. In the beginning, it is more important to create speed and see the results to keep motivation up than being able to encode your own images and reference stories, although ultimately this is the goal.

KEYS TO A GREAT MEMORY

▶ Encoding is used to convert information into memorable images that reference real information.

▶ Decoding is used to understand the meaning of images in a reference story (this is usually instant).

▶ Visual embedding is a process where you use the same sequence and pattern to encode a set of images, left to right or top to bottom.

▶ Narratives are a process of making information memorable by creating micro-stories, sometimes using something previously related to the word and changing the context.

▶ Aim to look for the value in what you are memorizing and use the Minimal Images Necessary (MIN) strategy to remember the information.

▶ Practise the dialling up technique to increase the intensity and memorability of your reference stories.

▶ Play with active daydreaming when you are looking for ways to create reference stories and tap into your creative unconscious resources.

5

The chain method: Build your capacity to remember

In this chapter you will learn:
- *benefits of using the chain method*
- *guiding principles to make information stick*
- *real-world examples of the chain method.*

The chain method is a core memory technique. It is quite probable that you have experienced it in one form or another or heard its name. If so, you may have already built up some associations and thoughts about its use, the challenges and practical applications.

In this chapter we will focus on the chain method's guiding principles and practical use and challenge you to 'search for where it can add value' within your own world.

Link by link

A major benefit of the chain method (sometimes referred to as the link system or link method) is that it allows you to take small chunks of related or non-related information and sequentially link them together for storage in mid- to long-term memory. This core technique extends the principle of reference stories. You might think of a chain method story as large reference stories anything between 10 and 20 images.

Insight

Essentially reference stories, link systems and chain methods are the same thing. I have referred to them by these names to help identify their purpose. I personally use the term 'reference story' for small chunks of information that are self-contained – a country and capital, English word and foreign equivalent, or a historic fact and date are examples of these. My preference for chain method stories is to remember lists of sequential items that won't change – chapters in a book or directions along a route, etc.

Action – Fact or fiction?

Time limit: 10 minutes

- ▶ Think about the natural process that happens when you read an engaging fictional book: how much do you remember? Do you recall the sequence of events? Details of the characters?
- ▶ Choose a fictional book that comes to mind and take three minutes to write down either in note form, pictures, story boards or on a mind map how much detail you can remember of it. Who were the characters? What was the plot? And so on...
- ▶ Now think back to the last factual book you read and write down as many details as you can.
- ▶ How were the experiences different? Did you find you remembered more of the fictional book in sequence or more details? In the factual book, if a key fact stood out, what was it about it that made it memorable?
- ▶ Capture your results and identify how you could make the factual book more memorable.

When you read the fictional book, chances are you were not making a conscious effort to remember. However, if the plot is vivid enough, it becomes instinctively more memorable, to the point where you can remember sequences of events in great detail. You are able to recall the experiences as if they were real and extract semantic information such as places, characters, dates and specific factual dialogue.

This is not always the way with a factual book: even if there is comprehension of semantic information, these facts can seem to fade from our memory. It is not linked to an experience, is probably difficult to remember in sequence or even at all until questioned later, at which time it may pop back into your mind if there was a strong enough meaning and association. One benefit of the chain method is the ability to create memorable experiences with semantic information.

The principles

There are some useful principles to abide by when using the chain method. These principles are within the context of the four core skills of creative memorization – relaxation, concentration, imagination and association.

SET THE BACKDROP

When you first start using the chain method, your chains can feel like they are floating in the ether of your mind, set against a backdrop of white or black, not connected to any specific location. Sometimes this can work, other times this can lead to similar images in different chains becoming confused, or just a general lack of clarity.

Just as you would set the backdrop within a book, a play or a movie, it helps to set the backdrop for the stories that you create in your mind. This backdrop can act as an anchor for the chains you create and a 'way in' to the story.

If I were to memorize the main topics in a book about programming, my backdrop may be the PHP conference I attended in California a few years back (note: although the backdrop is a point of reference, this is not the same as filing systems which we will discuss in the next chapter). I would perhaps imagine the story happening inside the hotel lobby or within a conference room or I may use the office I remember from the film *The Social Network*. I could even construct an imaginary stage (literally) within a theatre and on the stage are desks in a circle with laptops being powered by robots; this is where my story will take place.

Once my backdrop is set, I prime myself to think about the backdrop whenever I think about the book. I do this with some simple visualization and repetition – see the book, think about the backdrop, see the book, think about the backdrop, repeat this for about 60 seconds and the two are interlinked. Once the backdrop is primed, I am ready to create my chain of links.

HOW BIG SHOULD THE CHAIN BE?

The length of the chain depends on the type of information, your proficiency and how memorable you make it. Short chains – five links work well, however, you can just as easily use 10 or 20 if the information is contained and doesn't change. You should experiment and find out what works well for you.

Once you start – don't stop! Drive forward...

When you begin creating your links, focus on speed initially, build up a sense of rhythm and do not over-analyse. If you try to perfect each image before moving on, or have everything make sense, you are likely to get tired or lose motivation. When the information is more complex, this can lead to reverting back to simple rote memorization.

> **Insight**
>
> Most people will have experienced this state at some point in their lives, when a person is in the 'state of flow', perhaps playing a sport, giving a presentation, playing a blinding shot on a pool table or on the tennis court or coming up with a new idea in a meeting that everyone starts going along with. If you have experienced this in the past, you will remember that you have a feeling of just going with it, of momentum – this is the feeling that you want to let happen when using creative memorization and in this context the chain method.

DIALLING UP THE INTENSITY

This is the same technique used in the previous chapter: use your dial to intensify the experience and create vibrant, alive images and experiences.

WATCH THE MOVIE

Once you have completed all the links in your chain and you have a story built up in your mind, run it through as if you were either watching a movie or in the movie. Play it forward about 5–10 times, building up a sense of rhythm, intensifying the experience and involving all of your senses. Once you are confident with the sequence, press rewind and run the movie backwards, experiencing everything in reverse.

Fast forward and rewind

When you are happy that you can play the story in both directions, take it to the next level and hit fast forward and fast rewind. Run it forwards and backwards on high speed for 1–2 minutes. By running these patterns in this way, you will help strengthen the synaptic connections and create a solid chain.

ACT OUT!

This is where you get to actively test the information you have memorized. It is an essential step, especially when remembering speeches or presentations. As you watch the movie, narrate the real information, feel free to dramatize this – use physical gestures as if you were giving a speech to an audience or telling the story to a group of children. Recite the information in different genres – as if you were telling a horror, a drama, a comedy, a melodrama. Play with it and make it your own.

REVISION

Revision is important to condition the connections you have made, as mentioned in the first chapter. The suggested pattern for this is one hour after initial memorization, then one day, one week, one month, three months, six months, then as needed. In real terms the amount of revision will depend on the importance of the material and how you use it, along with how strong your initial connections are.

Insight

In the beginning make a conscious effort to apply all the guiding principles. If you do this, in time it will start to happen naturally. By working in this way, you will build up good habits and a solid foundation, allowing you to use your skills for more complex information.

Building the chain

If chain methods and reference stories are going to be useful to you in your life, your brain and, more specifically, your neurons need to get used to creating these types of pattern, so you no longer have to consciously think about 'how' you might create a connection and your unconscious can just throw out ideas and do the hard work for you.

On starting the journey to building up these patterns of a new way of thinking, work through these 'actions', creating your own links wherever possible.

Action – Ten elements

Time limit: 5 minutes
Follow the guiding principles to remember the first ten elements of the periodic table:

▶ Set the backdrop – perhaps you see a laboratory; the story below will happen with this backdrop. Throughout the story the backdrop may change to reflect the action.

> ▶ Create an image for each word in your mind (natural-image [n] and sound-image [s]):
>   1 Hydrogen – Bomb [n]
>   2 Helium – Balloon [n]
>   3 Lithium – Leaves [s]
>   4 Beryllium – Bee [s]
>   5 Boron – Boar [s]
>   6 Carbon – Car [s]
>   7 Nitrogen – Nitro [s]
>   8 Oxygen – Oxygen mask [n]
>   9 Fluorine – Toothpaste [n]
>   10 Neon – Neon strip [n]
> ▶ Make the images come alive; use your sense memory.
> ▶ Create your links to form a story using your imagination and association.

Example

You walk into the laboratory holding a Bomb and throw it into a hot air Balloon. As it rises and explodes, thousands of green Leaves fall to the ground covering a Bee (the size of a person), which stings a Boar. The boar runs at you and you manage to get into a Car before it smashes the door. You press the big button that says Nitro, you are going so fast around the laboratory an Oxygen mask drops down. When you stop, you take the huge tube of Toothpaste from the dashboard, step outside and squirt it onto a Neon strip.

▶ Dial up the intensity.
▶ Use the movie method.
▶ Act out! – The first few times you can recite the story you created. After that just recite the 'real' information – Hydrogen, Helium, Lithium, etc. while seeing the story in your mind.

Action – Book challenge

Time limit: 5 minutes

Here is an example of how you might use the chain method to quickly memorize the table of contents of a book. The book in this example is *Getting To Yes – Negotiating an agreement without giving in* by Roger Fisher and William Ury.

Here are the eight main content areas of the book, with examples of some images:

▶ Don't bargain over positions – lotus position
▶ Separate the people from the problem – people, problem blob
▶ Focus on interests, not positions – interesting sweets
▶ Invent options for mutual gain – invent options under three cups
▶ Insist on objective criteria – little critter
▶ Develop your BATNA (best alternative to negotiated agreement) – a BAT
▶ Negotiation Jujitsu – jujitsu
▶ Taming the hard bargainer – Taming

Remember to go through each stage of the guiding principles.

Insight

Try to have just one image representing each of the phrases. Before going on to create the chain method story, make sure you encode each of the sentences. When you see that Lotus position in your mind, you have to know that it means 'Don't bargain over positions'. This will make it a lot easier to recite the real information after you have linked together the whole chain.

Example

Reagan and Gorbachev are standing across from each other in the White House (my backdrop). I am sitting in a lotus position, they start fighting so I fly through the air and try to separate these people from a problem blob covering them. My focus is drawn to some interesting sweets stuck to the middle of Gorbachev's head. I grab the sweet and invent a game where I put the sweet under one of three cups, giving them options to choose from. An objective little critter jumps on top of cups and is holding a large metal bat, and starts hitting Reagan and Gorbachev, who join forces and do some jujitsu moves on the little critter, taming it and putting it back into its cage before shaking hands.

Insight

Although there is not a lot of detail here, this chain method story acts as a reference that lets me understand the essence of what the book is about. My brain will naturally reflect on information I already know about this subject and is primed for new input. Even without reading any more I, could have a conversation with someone about it and explore what I think each section means from my own experience. It will also clarify my purpose, i.e. What level of detail do I now want from this book? What are the key areas of interest for me? What will I do with this information?

In practice

> ### Action – *How to Remember Anything* chain method story
>
> **Time limit: 10 minutes**
> Preview the index of this book and extract a main key word for each chapter title and use the link system to form a chain that will act as your reference story for this book.
>
> Remember to use the core principles of creative memorization and go through each of the guiding principles of the chain method.

KEYS TO A GREAT MEMORY

▶ The chain method allows you to store potentially unrelated information in long-term memory.

▶ The chain method is like a long reference story.

▶ When using the chain method, put the information you are memorizing in context by giving it a backdrop.

▶ Aim to keep the size of your chain between 5 and 20 links.

▶ Create your links quickly and don't over-think; drive forward the momentum to keep your motivation levels high.

▶ Use the dialling up technique to intensify the memory of your chain.

▶ Practise 'Watching the movie' – run your chain forwards and backwards in your mind to consolidate it to long-term memory.

▶ Act out! Test that you remember all the information in your chain.

▶ Review your chains from time to time, one hour after memorization, then one day, one week, one month, as and when.

6

Memory networks: Your limitless mental storage systems

In this chapter you will learn:
- *how to organize your information through classification*
- *making information easier to remember by chunking*
- *how to store information in a structured manner*
- *techniques for creating limitless mental filing systems*
- *how to use mental filing systems in the real world.*

In this chapter you will discover how to use your skills to construct memory networks to store and retrieve an almost unlimited amount of information. Before digging into the workings of these techniques, it is beneficial to spend some time thinking about the classification and chunking of information.

Classification

> *'The action or process of classifying something according to similar qualities or characteristics.'*

One of the most challenging areas when starting a new job, learning a new subject or developing a new skill is knowing how to classify your information. Where do you start? What do you read? What do you need to learn and remember first? What is the best way to group the information? The answers to these questions will have an impact on 'what' you memorize, 'when' you memorize and 'how' you memorize. Your approach should involve classifying your information in line with your outcomes.

RECOGNIZING PATTERNS

For our purposes classification involves recognizing patterns that allow you to group similar information so it is easier to remember.

Think of the last time you walked into a bookshop. You immediately notice that the books have been classified into genres – fiction, science, children's, etc. Within those sections they are further classified alphabetically. This means that your brain can quickly identify those patterns within the shop; each genre has a specific location, making it easy to remember. If your outcome was to develop your management skills for the purpose of building a high-performing team, you may head to the business and self-development sections – there could be useful information in both these places.

SLICING

To help with recognizing patterns, a simple technique is to think of vertical and horizontal slices.

You might imagine a vertical slice being the table of contents within a book. If you were to memorize this, you would build up a big picture view of knowledge across the whole subject of the book.

You could imagine a horizontal slice consisting of one specific topic either within one book or across several books. To memorize this will increase the detail of knowledge on that one topic.

Let us visualize this in the context of a set of four books on memory improvement:

- ▶ *How to Remember Anything* (Mark Channon)
- ▶ *How to Pass Exams* (Dominic O'Brien)
- ▶ *Develop a Perfect Memory* (Tony Buzan)
- ▶ *Moonwalking with Einstein* (Joshua Foer)

Your purpose is to know as much about 'improving your memory' as possible, so you decide that you will take both vertical and horizontal slices from each book. The vertical slices will give you the big picture and the horizontal slices will give you the detail.

For each book the category for the vertical slice could be classified as the author. When you think of an author, you get back the name of the book along with the table of contents, topics and some main facts.

For each book you will have horizontal slices that could be classified by topics of interest. Let us say 'remembering names' was a topic you wanted to become an expert on. You extract details from each of the relevant chapters within the book and across all of the books; perhaps you also research what is on the internet and buy some more books giving more insights. This will build up a detailed view of that horizontal slice.

Both vertical and horizontal slices are done in the context of the learning cycle – you consume sensory information, reflect on what you know (which is increasing with each vertical or horizontal slice), abstract your own ideas and take action. You become excellent at remembering names and have a solid knowledge about improving your memory in general that you can use in your everyday life.

Of course you could just as easily choose to take a horizontal slice on its own. You want to remember names, so you consume a chapter from one book, reflect, abstract and put it into practice; this is a small horizontal slice. If you consume the chapters on names from four books, you have a bigger horizontal slice and potentially a more detailed view on that topic.

Thinking back to the bookshop analogy, your purpose was to learn about building a 'high performing team'. In this scenario you may take a horizontal slice from books across the two genres – business and self-development – extracting key information and creating your own classification called 'high-performing teams'.

As you will find out, we can create memory networks in our mind that mirror these classifications, building up storage structures for easy retrieval of information.

....

Insight

There can be a temptation with memory techniques to try to 'remember everything'. I've experienced this myself and your productivity can suffer. You don't have to remember 'everything'; however, you do want to remember 'anything' that will add value to your outcomes. If you already know something, don't waste time on rebuilding the memory with a memory technique. In this fast-paced world make the most of your time by classifying and remembering the things that allow you to be most effective.

....

Action – Classify me!

Time limit: 5 minutes
▶ Think about an area in which you wish to learn to develop your skills.
▶ What is most important for you to learn? What are you going to want to put into practice first? What is most important to you, and why?
▶ Reflect and abstract how you might slice up and classify this information.
▶ Write down or visually represent your findings.

Chunking

Once you have classified your information and are at a more granular level, you can start to look at the best way of organizing the information into bite-size chunks that are easier to remember and you can use for reference stories.

Chunking is a fairly simple concept and a way of taking a group of information and breaking it down so it can be more manageable for our working memory.

The classic example of this is a number: 241849382. On its own it seems pretty unwieldy to process; however, chunk it up and it is easier for your working memory to manage, i.e. 241, 849, 382 – you can hold these numbers in your mind long enough to work with them, think what they mean, how you might use them, etc.

Continuing with the bookshop analogy, if you extracted information from a chapter in, let's say, Ken Blanchard's *One Minute Manager* book *High Performing Teams*, you might take the chunk of information that represents what a high performing team looks like at a high level by memorizing the mnemonic PERFORM:

▶ Purpose
▶ Empowerment
▶ Relationships
▶ Flexibility
▶ Optimal performance

- ▶ Recognition
- ▶ Morale

You could also have a reference story (chain) to give a clearer picture of what the word PERFORM represents if it helps:

Imagine a PERFORMER with a real PURPOSE and super POWERS, in an intimate RELATIONSHIP with the OPTIMAL product (iPad), that has facial RECOGNITION and makes her feel GREAT.

Networks

Memory networks are a way of thinking about a group of systems that grew from the art of memory, allowing a structured approach to storing and retrieving the information you have classified.

A memory network is built up of unique nodes that follow a sequence and potentially point to other memory networks. The way you slice, classify and chunk your information will have an impact on how you construct your memory networks. As you continue to read, think about how you might construct your own.

There are a variety of memory networks. Here is a list of the most well-known:

- ▶ Peg lists – the body system, the rhyme system, the number shape system
- ▶ Method of loci – the journey method, the Roman room method (item system) or memory palace
- ▶ The major or phonetic system (also used for numbers).

They all follow the same process for storing information:

1 Identify a network of images (these are your nodes) that follow a sequence (parts of your body, pictures that rhyme with numbers, items in your home, locations along a route, etc.).
2 Memorize the sequence of your nodes.
3 Connect the information you want to remember to your nodes.

· ·

Insight
The term 'memory network' is not a 'new system'; it is merely a way of referring to any memory technique that allows you to mentally store information. My purpose here is to create a common language for us to

share the various applications of memory networks throughout the book. In the same way a 'node' can represent a location on a journey, an item in your home or a picture in a number shape system. Memory networks also conjure up imagery of neuronal networks in your mind with the idea that a memory network can mirror those internal synaptic connections.

THE PEG LIST

One of the simplest examples of a memory network is the peg list, the idea that you can 'hang' items off a virtual peg. In real terms you are simply creating an association between the peg (node) and the item you wish to remember.

The body system is a straightforward example of a peg list:

- ▶ Feet
- ▶ Knees
- ▶ Thighs
- ▶ Behind
- ▶ Waist
- ▶ Chest
- ▶ Neck
- ▶ Face
- ▶ Hair
- ▶ Ceiling

As you can see, it uses different parts of the body for visual pegs; associating information you wish to remember with each one of these images allows you to memorize rapidly and recall in or out of sequence.

Action – How to memorize a memory network

Time limit: 5 minutes
Memorization of a memory network is a simple process. The following steps you go through relate to all types of memory network:

1 Get yourself into a relaxed and focused state.
2 Imagine your first image vividly and say the name of the node aloud.
3 Repeat this process for each node of the memory network.

4 Now do this process in reverse.
5 Repeat steps 2–4 three times.
6 Chunk the files into smaller groups (1–5, for example).
7 Use the movie method – run through each group forwards and backwards in your mind as quickly as you can.
8 Use the movie method – run through the whole network forwards and backwards as quickly as you can until you are sure of the sequence in your memory network.

Action – 60-second challenge!

Time limit: 1 minute
First, memorize the body system using the process above.

Next put it into action by remembering some simple information. Associate the following ten items with the body's visual nodes. Try to do this within 60 seconds – there are examples if needed but try your own first:

- ▶ Feet and Glass
- ▶ Knees and Phone
- ▶ Thighs and Light bulb
- ▶ Behind and Candle (ouch!)
- ▶ Waist and Boat
- ▶ Chest and Ice cream
- ▶ Neck and Spanner
- ▶ Face and Statue
- ▶ Hair and Spaghetti
- ▶ Ceiling and Plant

Reference story examples
- ▶ Huge hairy feet stepping on glass
- ▶ A red shiny phone tying your knees together and ringing loudly
- ▶ Light bulbs attached to your thighs flashing on and off
- ▶ A candle burning your behind
- ▶ An elaborately designed boat sailing around your waist
- ▶ Freezing ice-cream poured over your chest
- ▶ A big metal spanner attaching bolts to your neck

- ▶ Your face is made out of marble like a statue
- ▶ Your hair is made out of spaghetti, with lots of sauce
- ▶ Tropical plants are growing from the ceiling

Notice how the reference stories engage your senses: your feet are not just made of glass, they are also huge and hairy. This will engage your senses which will in turn make the image instantly more memorable. The same applies to the phone, being shiny and ringing loudly.

CLEANING A MEMORY NETWORK

You may have memory networks that you use repeatedly for simple tasks. You could think of these as temporary memory networks, i.e. they have not been designed with a specific purpose of storing key information you wish to transfer to your long-term memory. With such a memory network you do not want to store the information any longer than is needed to complete your task.

If we use the simple example of storing a list of 'things to do', once you have completed the list you have no more use for this information. By simply leaving the memory networks for a few days, you will find that the images fade considerably; this is mainly due to the fact that when you memorized them, your intention was only to keep them for a short period of time, therefore your connections were less intense and therefore less memorable. After a few days you can go ahead and use the same system to store similar types of information.

There are times when images get 'stuck' or maybe you want to use the same memory network before the images have had time to fade. In this scenario there is a way of dulling down and erasing the information you associate with your files.

To clean a memory network, create an eraser image; this could be cellophane, for example, it is clear and has a feeling of nothingness, and gives the effect of erasing. Wrap the cellophane around each one of your files and say the word 'erase'.

RHYME LIST AND NUMBER SHAPE SYSTEM

Other peg lists include the rhyme list and number shape system; these also have some simple applications when it comes to remembering numbers, which we will look at in a later section.

Steps in creating a rhyme list and number shape system

Simply create an image that rhymes with each number from 0 to 10:

0 Hero
1 Bun
2 Shoe
3 Tree
4 Door
5 Hive
6 Sticks
7 Heaven
8 Plate
9 Wine
10 Hen

For the number shape system create an image that looks like the number:

0 Polo
1 Pencil
2 Swan
3 Bum
4 Sail
5 Hook
6 Bag
7 Nose
8 Track
9 Balloon
10 Laurel & Hardy

Action – Your daily meetings

Time limit: 5 minutes

An application of these systems is in helping to remember the order of your daily meetings. The value of this will of course depend on how busy you are.

Although this information can be stored on your phone, tablet or laptop, having this knowledge at your fingertips can create a sense of certainty and control in knowing what is coming up next, especially if you are working back to back.

Ideally you would take five minutes at the beginning of each day to memorize the sequence of meetings.

Memorize the following fictitious meetings:

- ▶ Catch up with one of your team members
- ▶ A project review with your manager
- ▶ Phone call with a potential client
- ▶ Meeting with a designer over new designs of your website
- ▶ Lunch with a colleague
- ▶ Your monthly stakeholder meeting
- ▶ Offsite meeting in Starbucks
- ▶ Email catch-up
- ▶ Work on an idea for a new project
- ▶ Business dinner at local restaurant (or pub)

Daily meetings example
Imagine the scenario in the location that it is happening and associate the rhyme list images or number shape images – take no more than two minutes. This technique can be done at high speed as the associations are fairly simple.

- ▶ *Your team member is eating a massive **bun**.*
- ▶ *Your manager is in the room where you are meeting him wearing massive clown **shoes** (this may also change your perception and your state).*
- ▶ *Your potential client is on the phone up a **tree**.*
- ▶ *Your designer is painting the **door** of the location where you are meeting him.*
- ▶ *You are having lunch with your colleague surrounded by **bees**.*
- ▶ *In your stakeholder meeting they are all holding big **sticks**!*
- ▶ *Imagine an **angel** in Starbucks.*
- ▶ *You are catching emails on your **plate** at your desk.*
- ▶ *Pouring **wine** over your new project.*
- ▶ *At dinner with lots of **hens**.*

By taking a few minutes each day to create some simple associations, you can remain focused and make sure you are prepared for the next meeting. The value of this technique will vary, depending on your career.

Insight

You will notice that I haven't added any times to these meetings. Since meetings are generally either 30 minutes or one hour, sometimes this is not needed. If you want to add in times, the upcoming number systems are ideal for this type of scenario. If using the above method, I would recommend alternating between the rhyme list and number shape system daily. This will allow the images to fade.

THE METHOD OF LOCI

The method of loci follows the simple principle of associating information you wish to remember with well-known 'locations' throughout some kind of journey; the locations are your 'nodes'.

The nodes may be simple items in your home, as with the Roman room method and memory palace, or points of focus on a journey from your home to work, sometimes referred to as the journey system. It may also be a combination of both.

In the following sections you will create three different memory networks using the method of loci. The first will use the Roman room method or memory palace, the second will use the journey method and the third will be one of your choice.

You will put these memory networks into practice at the end of this chapter by memorizing 60 key management models.

Action – Creating your memory palace

Time limit: 5 minutes
Create 20 locations using a memory palace (also known as Roman room method).

▶ To create a memory palace, you first need to choose a place that is your palace. For this action I would suggest you choose your home.
▶ Imagine you enter through the front door of your home (your memory palace). As you walk through your palace, 'note' the first four rooms you come to and their sequence.
▶ From each room within your palace you are going to choose just five items. Imagine picking the first item on your left and

looking around the room in a 'clockwise' direction, choose the next four items that follow in sequence – these items are your visual 'nodes' – you may have something like: chair, curtains, table, TV and bookcase.

► Choose five items from each room.
► Write the rooms and items in the table below.

Room 1	Room 2
1	6
2	7
3	8
4	9
5	10

Room 3	Room 4
11	16
12	17
13	18
14	19
15	20

Use the steps in *How to Memorize a Memory Network* in the 'Action' box from earlier in this chapter.

A memory palace doesn't have to be in your home; you could use your office, a bar or restaurant – as long as you have a room, all you have to do is select items from that room in a clockwise order as your visual nodes. Don't worry about knowing what the numbers are; the important thing is to remember their sequence.

THE JOURNEY METHOD

The journey method is another name for a memory network that utilizes the method of loci. Its advantage over some other memory networks is that you can generally construct very large networks and therefore hold a lot of information while still memorizing at a high speed.

It is based on the principle of selecting different locations as your visual nodes along a particular journey. You pick a starting location and a finishing location, and then choose as many locations in between as you can think of. The locations themselves can be anything – a room, a hallway, a garden, the corner of a street, a bus stop, a bus or a tree in a park; basically your location is any area of space that you can instantly recognize. It is important that you focus on a particular point at each location.

An example of a 'journey' might be a journey from your home to your work. You do not need to remember the numbers of your nodes, just the order in which they appear. Let's take a look at a hypothetical illustration:

- ▶ Home
- ▶ Garden
- ▶ Car
- ▶ Corner with a lamp
- ▶ Fence
- ▶ Chemist
- ▶ Roundabout
- ▶ Tesco
- ▶ Train entrance
- ▶ Inside station
- ▶ Tube stairs…

You will continue creating locations until you get to your office.

Insight

I find that the best way to create a new journey is to choose the start and end points; you can then take your journey and fill in the gaps. If you need a total of 50 locations and you end up with only 30, you can go back through the journey looking for locations you might have missed out. For example, there may have been a newsagent in between 'inside station' and the 'tube stairs', so you could add this in. If needed, you can extend the journey – office to coffee shop, etc.

Action – Building a journey

Time limit: 5 minutes
Create 30 locations using the journey method. You may find that you end up with many more locations than that. It is all right if you do; for the 'Action' towards the end of this chapter we shall just use the first 30.

- ▶ Name your journey – if it is a journey from home to work, call it home–work.

> ▶ Choose your start and end locations.
> ▶ Take no more than 10 minutes to brainstorm all of the locations in between. Make your locations as close together as possible as this will make for easier memorization.
> ▶ Use the steps in *How to Memorize a Memory Network* in the 'Action' box from earlier in this chapter.
>
> You can create as many journeys as your imagination and memory will allow; you may want to think of journeys you have taken throughout your life – to your school or college, to old places of work, airports, restaurants, places on holidays or trips to beaches. There are literally thousands of locations you could create.

Insight

Over the years I have noticed that creating memory networks has become a blocker for many people. They feel challenged thinking about new journeys, or simply feel they don't have the time. Using Google Maps streetview is a great way to rapidly create almost limitless memory networks.

In practice

THE KEY MANAGEMENT MODELS

The application of memory networks is invaluable: they allow you to memorize high volumes of information and at high speed. The speed at which you can memorize information makes them an essential and practical tool when it comes to helping you to progress your career through education or in business.

In order to understand how to put your memory networks into use and to demonstrate the value of working with them, the next 'Action' will get you to use the three filing systems you have created to remember the 60 key management models from Assen, Berg and Pietersma's *Key Management Models*. We will classify the management models into strategic, tactical and operational; we will need the following number of nodes (files):

▶ 18 files to remember the strategic models in the first system
▶ 29 files to remember the tactical models in the second system
▶ 12 files to remember the operational models in the third system.

Taking a vertical slice from the book, you will memorize the names of each of these models.

In order to comprehend how these models work, you have to experience them and put them into practice. By remembering the names of each of the management models you are effectively creating points of reference within your mind for each of the models.

....

Insight

When I first memorized these models, it took only 60 minutes to commit the names of the models to memory – it took a further two weeks playing with each model to understand it. This is a relatively short space of time and for me has value. I noticed from a leadership point of view to have Covey's seven habits as a reference was invaluable when working with my team. It may be that you choose the models that are most relevant to you. What is your top ten that you can use to help make an impact in your career?

....

Strategic models

Memory network node (location)	Sensory information management model	Integrate reference story (examples)
	Ansoff's product / market grid	Ants on a market
	The BCG matrix	Boston red soxs Consulting
	Blue ocean strategy	Blue Ocean
	Competitive analysis: Porters five forces	A hand with five fingers being competitive
	Core competencies	Apple core
	Greiner's growth model	Grinding a model
	Kay's distinctive capabilities	Kay is very distinctive
	Market-driven organization	A market driving
	Off-shoring / outsourcing	Off-shore shipping truck

(continued)

Memory network node (location)	Sensory information management model	Integrate reference story (examples)
	Road-mapping	A road map
	Scenario planning	A crazy scenario
	Strategic dialogue	Two very strategic people having dialogue
	Strategic HRM model	Human Resources making models
	Strategic human capital planning	Humans on the capital planning
	SWOT analysis	A SWATter
	The value chain	Expensive valuable chain
	Value-based management	Valuable basin with management inside
	The value disciplines of Treacy and Wiersema	Dick Tracy Fears Semolina

Tactical models

Memory network node (location)	Sensory information management model	Integrate reference story (your stories)
	The 7-S framework	
	Activity-based costing	
	Beer and Nohria – E and O theories	
	Benchmarking	
	Business process redesign	
	Competing values of organizational effectiveness	
	Core quadrants	

(*continued*)

Memory network node (location)	Sensory information management model	Integrate reference story (your stories)
	Covey's seven habits of highly effective people	
	Curry's pyramid: customer marketing and relationship management	
	The DuPont analysis	
	Factory gate pricing	
	Henderson and Venkatraman's strategic alignment model	
	Hofstede's cultural dimensions	
	House of purchasing and supply	
	The innovation circle	
	Kotler's 4Ps of marketing	
	Kotler's eight phases of change	
	Kraljic's purchasing model	
	Lean thinking / just-in-time	
	MABA analysis	
	Milkovich's compensation model	
	Mintzberg's configurations	

(*continued*)

Memory network node (location)	Sensory information management model	Integrate reference story (your stories)
	Monczka's purchasing model	
	Overhead value analysis	
	Quick response manufacturing	
	Senge – the fifth discipline	
	Six sigma	
	The EFQM excellence model	
	The theory of constraints	
	Vendor managed inventory	

Operational models

Memory network node (location)	Sensory information management model	Integrate reference story (your stories)
	The balanced scorecard (BSC)	
	Belbin's team roles	
	The branding pentagram	
	Change quadrants	
	Discounted cashflow	
	Kaizen / Gemba	
	Mintzberg's management roles	

(*continued*)

Memory network node (location)	Sensory information management model	Integrate reference story (your stories)
	Risk reward analysis	
	Root cause analysis / Pareto analysis	
	The six thinking hats of de Bono	
	The Deming cycle: plan-do-check-act	
	Value stream mapping	

Insight

The method of loci memory networks are extremely effective once you have had time to practise with them. They can be used in isolation or combined together to create more complex networks. The inside of shops along a street could be used to hold main chapters of a book and items within those shops could be used for details of that chapter. You can use it to remember an almost limitless variety of things - dance steps, speeches, books, even games for the World Memory Championships; with it I was able to memorize a pack of cards in 1min 24 sec (unofficial time), the current record holder Simon Reinhard can do the same thing in 19 seconds.

KEYS TO A GREAT MEMORY

▶ Look for patterns when classifying your information, finding items with similar qualities.

▶ Slicing is an easy way to think about classifying your information, a vertical slice gives you the big picture while a horizontal slice gives you the detail on a topic or theme.

▶ Practise chunking information into bite-size portions so it is more manageable for your working memory.

▶ Memory network is a term used to represent a group of systems that allow a structured approach to storing and retrieving information.

▶ Some key memory networks include peg lists, method of loci and the major system.

▶ You can clean your memory networks by creating an eraser image.

▶ Use the rhyme list and number shape system to remember daily meetings.

▶ Get into the habit of creating memory networks, aim to build a new network once a week to begin with.

▶ Take advantage of Google Maps for a limitless source of memory networks.

7

The number system: Learn the value of remembering numbers

In this chapter you will learn:
- *the benefits of having a memory for numbers*
- *how to create a visual vocabulary for numbers*
- *temporary and permanent number systems*
- *when to use the right techniques for the right purpose*
- *how to set up a framework for statistics.*

What's in a number?

Within the context of your career, remembering numbers could play a big role: for many it is an invaluable skill. This goes much further than showing off at parties or memorizing all the phone numbers in your contacts list; while impressive, in this day and age, most of this information is stored and easily accessible via your phone and backed up in 'the cloud'.

The real value in being able to remember numbers will vary for each individual depending on your career. If you have your own business, are involved in running projects or products, work in marketing, sales, law or perhaps politics, then the ability to pull key dates, figures and statistics out of your head is a very powerful technique. It demonstrates your knowledge and sets you up as a person of knowledge in your area, showing that you are up with the latest trends. Most likely it will also make you the go-to person and allow you to influence meetings and negotiations. If none of the above apply to you, there will be some key areas in your life where the ability to remember numbers will make a difference.

> **Insight**
> Having worked as a product manager at the BBC, I have experienced first-hand benefit in being able to reel off the latest figures and statistics, not only for the product I was delivering but also for our competitors.

> **Action – Numbers in your world**
>
> **Time limit: 5 minutes**
> ▶ Identify the key areas in your life where having the ability to memorize numbers would benefit you in some way, start with your personal life then think about your current job and finally move on to focusing on your future career. Imagine the skills you would need to achieve some of your future goals.
> ▶ Take five minutes to capture these thoughts.

A new vocabulary

The concept of making numbers memorable uses the same four core skills of creative memorization. In the same way that we use sound-images, natural-images and reference stories that refer to real-world information, for numbers we create a visual vocabulary of number-images that refer to a set of numbers.

RHYME LIST AND NUMBER SHAPE SYSTEM

Before looking at a more complex system, there are two very easy number systems that allow you to remember numbers. You are already familiar with these systems after working with them in the previous chapter – the rhyme list and the number shape system. Although their application is limited, they are a good introduction to the concept of creating a visual vocabulary for numbers.

> **Action – Remember your PINs**
>
> **Time limit: 5 minutes**
>
> *Steps*
> We will use visual embedding in this example.

Credit card PIN: 3801 – we use rhyme list and number shape system alternately, so 3801 would be Tree (3), Track (8), Hero (0), Pencil (1). Rather than create a narrative for this one you may use some simple visual embedding:

▶ Imagine you are in a room in your home. Your credit card is the same size as you. See it in every detail (use sense memory). Now on a table or the floor create the four images for each digit – again use sense memory to make them real.
▶ The credit card has four positions where you can embed these images; these will always follow the same order – on top, on the side, through the middle, on the bottom.
▶ Imagine the tree embedded in the top like a head, there are two tracks embedded in each side like arms, a hero is embedded in the middle like a belt, pencils are on the bottom like feet.
▶ Zoom into each image and use your sense memory to experience it in detail.
▶ Now take a step back and see the credit card with the tree, tracks, hero and pencils as one image.
▶ As you look at the image say 'Hi credit card, your number is 3801', then touch his head, shake his hand, straighten his belt and clean his shoes.

By doing the above you are engaging different neuronal pathways to remember one bit of information, which will make it much more likely to transfer it into long-term memory.

Ultimately we want to devise a visual vocabulary that will allow us to remember long sequences of numbers. The process of devising this visual vocabulary can be done in many different ways. While the rhyme system and number shape system could potentially fill this purpose, with anything over single digits they are not very practical.

Ideally we need an image for every two-digit number from 00 to 99: this way we can have the ability to remember a range of different number sequences.

You could attempt to do this through natural images, for example:

▶ The number 13 could be a **black cat**
▶ The number 18 is a **key**

- ▶ The number 88 is a **fat lady**
- ▶ The number 10 is the **prime minister**
- ▶ The number 64 is **Georgina the Giraffe** from 64 Zoo Lane

If you can think up 100 different images to represent all the numbers from 00 to 99, this is a pretty good place to start. However, it can be quite a challenging task.

Insight

It is not necessary to have an elaborate system in order to create your number-images. The example above can be really useful for children and could as easily work for adults. When working with children, I create an image for each group of 10 (10 is Hen, 20 is Penguin, 30 is Snake); these are all arbitrary and worked out with whatever the children come up with. I then combine these images with the rhyme list, so 33 would be a Snake (30) wrapped around a Tree (3) – I usually introduce them to this system when learning times tables so there is a practical application for it.

THE MAJOR SYSTEM

The major system allows you to create a complete visual vocabulary for numbers. It uses a code in order to construct a number-image for each two-digit number from 00 to 99 (you can also use it to construct three- and four-digit numbers; we will focus on two here, though). There are several other systems out there that do the same thing in different ways: many people, especially memory athletes, have created their own systems to memorize thousands of consecutive digits in competition. Once you understand the concepts, you may find you want to create your own system.

Insight

In the 1995 World Memory Championships, I used the major system to remember 732 consecutive digits in one hour. This was using the basic system: all in all I memorized about 400 images in the hour. Current memory athletes have more advanced systems than I used back then, allowing them to create an image that represents six digits rather than two. At the time of writing this book, the world record for most digits memorized in an hour is held by World Memory Champion Wang Feng with an astounding 2,280 digits.

For simplicity and understanding we will focus on the major system – as well as numbers, once you learn the major system it can come in very useful with creating mnemonic codes for other types of information which we will explore in Chapter 13 *Information overload*.

With enough practice you will be able to look at any number between 00 and 99 and instantly have an image to represent it.

How it works
This major system has a code based on the principle that each number from 0 to 9 has a phonetic sound or sounds associated with it (we will refer to this as the major system code). From these sounds you can create words (images). The end result is that you build a vocabulary of images that represent numbers.

The following represents the phonetic sounds associated with each number from 0 to 9:

▶ 0 are the sounds that the letters Z and S make, as in Zorro and Snake
▶ 1 are the sounds that the letters T and D make, as in Teddy and Diamond
▶ 2 is the sound the letter N makes, as in Nuts
▶ 3 is the sound the letter M makes, as in Mike
▶ 4 is the sound the letter R makes, as in Rat
▶ 5 is the sound the letter L makes, as in Light
▶ 6 are the sounds the letters J, Sh and Ch make, as in Jam, Ship and Chips
▶ 7 are the sounds the letters K, G and NG make, as in Cat, Gun and riNG
▶ 8 are the sounds the letters F and V make, as in Fire and Van
▶ 9 are the sounds the letters P and B make, as in Pea and Bite

The sounds **A, E, I, O, U, W, H, Y** have no value. These no-value sounds enable us to create words.

It is important to note that it is **not the name** of the letter but the **sound of the letter** that equates to the number, so the word CeDaR would actually be the number 014, not 714, because the sound the C makes is S as in 'see'.

Example

▶ *22 could be NuN – N = 2, U has no value, N = 2*
▶ *37 could be MaC – M = 3, A has no value, C = 7*
▶ *59 could be LaB – L = 5, A has no value, B = 9*

Action – Learning the major system code

Time limit: 15 minutes

Use the following natural associations to remember the sounds associated with each number from 0 to 9. With repetition you will soon know these off by heart.

1 From a phonetic point of view, each group of sounds is created in the same part of the mouth.
   - Z and S, for example, are made behind the teeth at the front of the mouth.
   - T and D are made at the top and front of the mouth by the tongue.
   - J, Sh and Ch are again made at the front of the mouth and form the same shape.
   - K, G and NG are made by the tongue at the back of the mouth.
   - F and V are made with the top teeth and bottom lip.
   - P and B are made with the lips.
2 Spend a few minutes saying each group of sounds and notice where you make them in your mouth; by doing this the natural associations will make more sense for you.
3 Visualize the following natural associations and repeat them out loud, noticing the part of the mouth you are using. Run through this 5–10 times until you feel comfortable that you can recall the sound for each number.
   - 0 starts with the sound Z
   - 1 has 1 downstroke like T and D
   - 2 has 2 downstrokes like N
   - 3 looks like an M if you turn it on its side
   - 4 – the last sound in four is R
   - 5 digits on your hand; when you look at your palm with your thumb pointing to the side, it forms the letter L
   - 6 flipped over resembles the letter J
   - 7 stuck back to back forms the letter K
   - 8 can look like a handwritten F
   - 9 can look like a P or B

All of these associations will be temporary as after a short amount of time and practice you will just 'know' what sounds the numbers make.

Action – Find the number

Time limit: 5 minutes

Deconstruct this table of words into their correct numbers.
Remember it is the sound the word makes that represents its
number, not the letter, so a word such as 'mummy' would be 33,
not 333; similarly a word such as 'cage' would be 76, not 77.

lab	duck	bin	fish	cape
mayor	roar	tail	can	phone
chief	shot	sail	net	leaf
beer	map	bash	nag	leach

The major system number matrix

In the following table you can see an example of a number matrix
created using the major system. Each of these images represents an
image from 00 to 99. These are not the only images you could use.
Using the major system, 65 could just as easily be Cello (sounds like
'chello') or Agile (sounds like 'ajile').

There is a learning curve in creating your own number matrix;
however, if you have identified your purpose there is real value in it
and therefore major benefits.

MAJOR SYSTEM NUMBER MATRIX EXAMPLE

00	01	02	03	04	05	06	07	08	09
Sauce	Sit	Sin	Sam	Soar	Sail	Sash	Sack	Safe	Zip
10	11	12	13	14	15	16	17	18	19
Daisy	Data	Dan	Dam	Door	Doll	Dash	Duck	Toffee	Tap
20	21	22	23	24	25	26	27	28	29
Noose	Net	Nun	Nam	Nero	Nail	Nash	Nag	Knife	Nappy
30	31	32	33	34	35	36	37	38	39
Mace	Mat	Minnie	Mummy	Marry	Mail	Mash	Mag	Mafia	Mop
40	41	42	43	44	45	46	47	48	49
Race	Rat	Rain	Rum	Roar	Rail	Rash	Rake	RAF	Rope
50	51	52	53	54	55	56	57	58	59
Lace	Lead	Alien	Lamb	Lara	Lilly	Lash	Lake	Leave	Lab
60	61	62	63	64	65	66	67	68	69
Jaws	Shot	Chain	Jam	Chair	Chilli	Gigi	Chuck	Chief	Chap

70	71	72	73	74	75	76	77	78	79
Case	Cat	Can	Gum	Car	Claw	Cash	Cake	Café	Cap

80	81	82	83	84	85	86	87	88	89
Vase	Fat	Vine	Foam	Fur	Fool	Fish	Fag	Viva	Phoebe

90	91	92	93	94	95	96	97	98	99
Boss	Bat	Bin	Beam	Beer	Bill	Bash	Bag	Beef	Poppy

Insight

I find it extremely useful to create two images for each two-digit number. This is more advanced and utilized by many memory athletes. For each two-digit number, you can create a Person and an Object – for 49 I may have a Cowboy and a Rope, for 94 I may have Homer Simpson drinking beer. This allows me to combine the person from one number with the object of another – 4994 would be a Cowboy drinking Beer and 9449 would be Homer Simpson with a Rope. You can take this one step further and have a Person–Action–Object for each two-digit number: this takes some crafting and is probably only really useful if you intend to compete in memory competitions or are memorizing a lot of numbers in your career.

Action – Memorizing the number matrix (part 1)

Time limit: 30 minutes

▶ First construct your own number matrix using the major system.
▶ Create a table like the one above and write down words that make sense for you.
▶ Spend some time reading the words you have written and making sure you can decode them back into numbers.
▶ Get someone to give you one of the words you have written and tell them what the number is.

Action – Memorizing the number matrix (part 2)

Time limit: 30 minutes

In order to speed up the process of remembering your images, use a combination of a small memory network (10 nodes) and the chain method:

▶ Create a small memory network with 10 nodes (perhaps a simple journey).

- Use the chain method to memorize the images you have created for the numbers 00–09. This will allow you to refer to your number matrix without looking at the table you have created and create stronger synaptic connections.
- *Example – You are holding a giant bottle of sauce (00) while you sit (01) in a house of sin (02) with Sam (03) and soar (04) through space, powered by an atomic sail (05) made of a red satin sash (06) but you crash into a sack (07) and get locked in a safe (08) that is closed by a zip (09).*
- Do the same for each group, 20–29 and so on up to 90–99

THE SEVEN-DAY CHALLENGE

Over the next seven days spend ten minutes running through the matrix in your mind saying the numbers out loud as you see the images in your mind. Pay attention to any numbers you notice during your day and think how this would be represented as one of your images.

With practice the images that represent the numbers will become second nature; to be really effective you need to get to the stage where you no longer encode or decode the numbers and images; you just know that 24 is Nero or whatever image you choose to create. When this happens, remembering numbers is as easy as remembering a set of images.

Action – 100 digits

Time limit: 15 minutes

This 'Action' will help to familiarize you with your new number matrix. Feel free to refer to the number matrix you have written down, as you may not have memorized it yet.

- Create a memory network with 20 nodes (a journey with 20 locations).
- Memorize the following 40 digits by associating one image with a location.
- *Example*
  If your first location is your living room, or an item in your living room, and the first two digits are 92, you will associate bin with your living room; the next two digits will be associated on your next file, and so on throughout the rest of the number.
- 9201982547 3847509377 5419152430 9607927152

Temporary or permanent

Depending on your purpose, the visual vocabulary you develop for your matrix may not fit every situation. At times when you have to memorize a number at high speed, the matrix of pre-determined images you create can be extremely beneficial. In some situations, especially when expanding your knowledge on a subject, it can be more beneficial to craft an image that is more closely associated with the information, as with a fact and a date:

▶ Emancipation of the Serfs, 1861
▶ Serfs being FiSHeD (861) out of Russia and set free.
▶ You usually have a good idea of which millennium it was in, so you need an image only for the last three digits.

You could therefore think of two types of system, each with a specific purpose: temporary numbers that utilize your numbers matrix and permanent numbers that are hand-crafted images using the phonetic code to create a word that is closely associated with the information being memorized. The latter takes slightly longer as you have the challenge of creating a unique word; however, it is more easily transferred into long-term memory and therefore requires less repetition.

Insight

I like to use the matrix images I create specifically for either rapid memorization on the hoof, i.e. meeting room numbers, times, dates, statistics, etc., or mental workouts, demos, presentations and competitions. If, on the other hand, I wish to consolidate a number in my long-term memory, primarily general knowledge (history, entertainment, geography, etc.), anything with a fact and an associated date, I will generally construct a specific image using the major system code.

Action – Permanent numbers

Time limit: 15 minutes
Using the phonetic code, memorize the following inventions and the date they were invented using a specific image from the phonetic code:

Inventions	Reference story (examples)
Microscope – 1590	a microscope with huge red **LiPS**
Vacuum cleaner – 1901	vacuuming up **BiSTo** gravy granules
Pistol – 1540	a **LaRS** firing a pistol
Aeroplane – 1903	an aeroplane flying into a **BoSoM**

Inventions	Reference story (your stories)
Telescope – 1608	
Radar – 1904	
Glider – 1853	
Bicycle – 1861	
Electric battery – 1800	
Hot air balloon – 1709	

Insight

There is a useful piece of software available called 2Know, from www.got2know.net/, that allows you to type in a number and it automatically generates a number of images based on the phonetic code, allowing you to choose the most appropriate one. Of course, you need to know your code extremely well to be able to translate images back to numbers at speed, but this will come with time and practice.

In practice

SET UP A FRAMEWORK FOR STATISTICS

Previously we looked at filing systems and the ability to classify and store your reference stories and link systems in a way that makes them easily accessible to you. To demonstrate the benefit of recalling numbers, let us look at a potential real-world situation for remembering statistics.

This framework will allow you to keep historical data for this fictitious company stored in your mind and allow you to update at weekly intervals with the option to store off-the-cuff data or day-to-day updates for key meetings or presentations.

The fictitious company

MnemoCorp – a large and successful social network site offering the ability to share and comment on the latest to do with brain research, memory improvement and personal development. MnemoCorp have embedded social functionality allowing people to share their content.

KPIs (Key Performance Indicators)

The statistics they are capturing are:

▸ Numbers of shares per week
▸ Number of comments on those shares per week

Here is an example of some historical statistics over a four-week period:

21/03/2011–27/03/2011
Content shared: 23,576 – up 117%

Comments per share: 9 – up 19%

28/03/2011–03/04/2011
Content shared: 65,604 – up 178%

Comments per share: 9 – down 4.4%

04/04/2011–10/04/2011
Content shared: 89,054 – up 36%

Comments per share: 10 – up 8.1%

11/04/2011–17/04/2011
Content shared: 76,571 – down 14%

Comments per share: 6 – down 33%

The memory network

For this example you could construct a combination of the journey method and item system. There are 52 weeks in a year so 52 locations give you the ability to store a year's worth of data. Over time this will give you the ability to report on percentage increases month by month and per quarter, giving you different ways to report on the data.

Since you will be accumulating this data over a long period of time, it is not essential to create all 52 locations; you could start with four, allowing you to capture the past four weeks. If this were real, you would most likely create another four so you were prepared for the month ahead.

Let us imagine that there are four locations for four weeks: you will allocate the name of the month to each location and the date will be a number-image associated with the centre of that location. Each location will have four items (these are your nodes).

Example (you can make up your own nodes for the last three locations):

▶ *Coffee shop (March), number-image: NeT (21)*
▶ *Coffee machine, content shared: NaM (23), LuGGaGe (576) – Nam drinking coffee with his luggage*
▶ *Cake stand, up by: TooTHaCHe (117) – a cake with toothache*
▶ *Sofa, comments per share: SoaP (09) – a sofa covered in soap*
▶ *Chair: up by: DeBBie (19) – a chair with Debbie Reynolds dancing on it*
▶ *Marks and Spencer (March), number-image: NaVy (28)*
▶ *W.H. Smith (April), number-image: SoaR (04)*
▶ *Boots (April), number-image: DaTa (11)*

From the above we can see that the Coffee shop represents 21 March. Content shared is 23,576, up by 117%, and comments per share are 9, up by 19%.

Action – Memorizing statistics

Time limit: 30 minutes
Create your own nodes for each location.

Memorize the rest of the statistics.

Information	Reference story (your stories)
28/3	
65,604 – up 178%	
9 – down 4.4%	
4/4	
89,054 – up 36%	
10 – up 8.1%	
11/4	
76,571 – down 14%	
6 – down 33%	

- ▶ In w/c 28/3 was content shared up or down and by how much?
- ▶ In w/c 11/4 what was the amount of content shared, was this up or down on previous weeks?
- ▶ In what week was content shared at its highest?
- ▶ In w/c 4/4 what was the average comments per share?

Of course as the stats go up or down each week there will be a reason, a story that goes along with it; you can easily capture this story within your locations. For example, stats went down w/c 11/4 because the application that measures the statistics went offline for one day that week – you could imagine the application falling over, attached to a particular item in your location to represent this. Ultimately, the story behind the statistics is the thing that is really important, as this will give you knowledge about what is working and what is not.

> **Insight**
>
> Although you used only four nodes per location here, in a real-world situation I would suggest creating around ten nodes. The good thing is that you don't have to create that many in advance.

KEYS TO A GREAT MEMORY

▶ Identify the areas in your life where being able to remember numbers will add some value.

▶ To memorize numbers, create a visual vocabulary by constructing a set of number-images.

▶ Learn the major system code in order to turn any number into a memorable number-image.

▶ Allocate time to design your own number matrix for the numbers 00 to 99.

▶ Take the seven-day challenge and spend ten minutes a day mastering your number matrix.

▶ Practise hand-crafting permanent numbers for specific information.

8

Mind mapping: Create, capture, consume and communicate

In this chapter you will learn:
- *how mind maps reflect the way we think*
- *how to find your own style and own your mind maps*
- *step by step how to mind map*
- *to use mind maps to create, capture, consume and communicate.*

Mind maps are creative tools that allow a person to create, capture, consume and communicate. Although visual thinking has been around for thousands of years, Tony Buzan is the originator of mind maps.

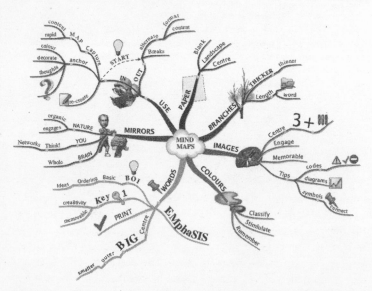

Figure 8.1 A mind map (created using ThinkBuzan'siMindMap http://www.thinkbuzan.com).

Mirror the mind

One of the core ideas behind mind mapping is that it mirrors the way we think. In the same way that our brain is constantly forming connections and pathways, mind maps capture and reflect some of those key associations we make in our mind.

On the surface, mind mapping can appear a simple process that produces an interesting way of capturing notes. Once you delve deeper into the mechanics of mind mapping, you start to see there are subtle complexities that can play a significant role in their effectiveness.

If you have used mind maps in the past, you may have had the same reaction that many people seem to have to Marmite – you love it or you hate it – 'you just get it' or 'it's just not how your mind works'. Both are valid perceptions. The main difference that a mind map has is that it capitalizes on more sensory inputs and therefore facilitates more opportunities to make connections to the information, whether you are brainstorming, taking notes in a meeting, learning information from a book or communicating your ideas to others.

Insight

I have been employing mind maps since the early 1990s. From my experience of working with many people over the years, those who say 'it's not how I work' have either misunderstood what a mind map is and usually produce something similar to a spider-gram or have got confused by 'rules'. My suggestion if yours was the latter experience is to wipe the slate clean and explore the ideas in this chapter as if you were seeing them for the first time, holding back any preconceived ideas and enjoying playing with the 'Actions'. Mind maps do require reconditioning of how you 'operate'; after all, most of us have been conditioned to write linear notes and create lists from an early age (they still have their use, by the way).

MIND MAPPING AND THE LEARNING CYCLE

Mind mapping naturally employs the learning cycle. As mentioned, it has many sensory inputs, allows you to reflect on the big picture and the details, creates an opportunity to abstract your own thoughts and take action through adding new branches, through rehearsal or through putting the information to use. The outcome of this is that your brain makes more connections to the information, which in turn makes the information more memorable.

If you used a mind map to learn a speech or presentation, once the message, outcomes, ideas and structure are in place, you complete the circle by putting it into action.

Act out! using the map as a prompt (we will go into detail on this in the section *The four Cs* below).

Action – Your current process

Time limit: 10 minutes
Before you begin, get either a notepad or paper and a pen.

Think back to a time (it can be recently) when you had to capture or consume some information: perhaps you were studying for an exam, taking notes in a meeting or learning new skills for work. As you remember this situation, write down:

► How did you capture your notes?
► How did you memorize these notes?
► How did you revise or review the information?
► How hard or easy was it to remember the information on a scale of 0–10?
► How long did you retain the information for?
► How have you captured the answer to these questions?

As you review what you have written, circle which of the following skills you believe you have put into practice:

Left brain dominant	Right brain dominant
Logic	Colour
Linearity	Dimension
Lists	Daydreaming
Sequence	Rhythm
Words	Imagination
Analysis	Gestalt (whole picture)
Numbers	Spatial awareness

Mind mapping, rather than using one set of skills more than another, incorporates all of these skills: words with colour, logic with imagination, sequence with rhythm, detail with the big picture.

Insight

When I first thought about this, I remembered note-taking at school (back in the 1970s/80s) and noticed that I scored high on the more dominant left-brain skills – logic, lists, sequence, words – and I would use repetition to drill it into my head. However, I hardly had anything on imagery, dimension, daydreaming (I would daydream but it wouldn't be connected to the stuff I was learning). My notes were, for the most part, black and white, nearly all in list format, sometimes pictures or diagrams, but they were never connected and I had no way of seeing the big picture. I could cram for exams but nothing 'stuck'.

In this sense, you could think of mind mapping as a whole-brain tool. Mind maps mirror the learning cycle and trigger activity throughout the brain, facilitating more connections.

Mind maps and you

Action – What's your style?

Time limit: 3 minutes

▶ Imagine that you are going into an interview situation or a meeting where you have to tell someone all about yourself: background, qualities, strengths, weaknesses, likes, loves, goals, etc. Thinking about involving as many of the skills we have previously mentioned as possible, spend just three minutes creating what you believe to be a mind map to reflect this information.

▶ Note: *There is no right or wrong answer here, the purpose of this action is merely to get you to start thinking about incorporating different cortical skills and finding your natural style.*

Insight

Visual note-taking is also a popular method of visual thinking; it has many similar qualities to mind mapping. I would liken it more to the chain method as it takes you on a journey. Since my focus has been in the mind mapping arena, I don't go into detail around visual note-taking here. There are some excellent resources and you can see some visual notes taken from a talk I did at SXSW in 2010 on this link – http://www.blog.imagethink.net/line-by-line/2010/3/12/memory-matters-at-sxsw.html by Heather Willems.

How to mind map

You don't have to be an artist to mind map or do visual note-taking. If you follow some simple guidelines, your mind maps will be extremely effective whether you wish to create, capture, consume or communicate.

> ## Action – The story of a mind map
>
> **Time limit: 15 minutes**
> Here are the steps to creating a mind map. As you read through the following, reflect back to the mind map picture at the beginning of the chapter, thinking about how you could create your own. We will assume you are mind mapping by hand.

Paper

- ▶ Whenever possible use 'blank' A3, A4 or A5 paper or whiteboard (avoid using lined paper as this imposes a linear structure).
- ▶ Use landscape orientation.
- ▶ Always start with a central image.

Branches

- ▶ Branches give the mind map its style; this is a big factor in a mind map catching your 'attention' and 'engaging' you.
- ▶ Be as creative as you like with what your branches look like; if you are creating a mind map to reflect music, then each branch could be an instrument.
- ▶ Work to give your mind map an organic look and feel as if it is a living organism, radiating and connecting, helping to bring information to life and therefore make it more memorable.
- ▶ The branch you use should only be as long as the word or image it supports; this allows those words and images to be closely connected, when you recall those words they will be associated spatially.
- ▶ The branches should avoid being linear; think of flowing movements or even use imagery to represent your branches.
- ▶ Connectors are branches that connect 'other' branches together; there are no hard and fast rules, however, it is recommended that the branches are in close vicinity, otherwise your mind map can

quickly turn into spaghetti junction. If you do use a connector that traverses your mind map, do so sparingly.

Images

▶ Imagery lies at the heart of your mind map.

▶ Always start with the central image; if it is text then make it 3D.

▶ Give your central image at least three colours (if you are capturing at high speed, this may not be possible).

▶ Images should be used across your map to make information memorable and stand out, or sum up a complex idea in one picture; the old adage 'A picture speaks a thousand words' is especially true with a mind map.

▶ Think of codes as images that tell you something about the word on the branch; it may draw special attention to it or give the word a higher priority.

▶ Symbols are similar to codes, but they differ in their purpose: whereas codes give specific meaning to a branch, symbols tell the story of relationships between branches.

> ▶ There is a *Pin* on the *Symbols branch* and on the *Words branch* – this implies that 'symbols' *connect* 'words'.

> ▶ The light bulb on the branch *BOI* (Basic Ordering Ideas – these are the words on your Level 1 Branches – PAPER, BRANCHES, IMAGES, COLOURS, WORDS, MIRRORS, USE) also appears on the connector line *Start* – the relationship here is that whenever we USE a mind map to take information in or get information out we should start with *BOI* wherever possible

▶ Diagrams and charts are used in many situations, by bringing your Powerpoint chart into a mind map you can show where it connects to the Big Picture (this is especially useful with mind map software).

▶ Over time you will start to build your own vocabulary for codes and symbols, a common language that will help you create quicker and stronger connections with new information.

Colours

▶ Use colours to classify the information and ideas on your mind map (you may use colour already to do this – colour-coding sections of a folder or using highlighters to make specific points stand out). This helps identify structures within the map. Colour is a simple way of attracting attention to information with similar qualities.

▶ There are usually emotional connections to colour (blue feels cool or cold, yellow feels warm and sunny, etc.); this can help to stimulate your imagination and inspire imagery.

- There are some great books that demonstrate the difference colour makes with regard to how much you can remember. *The Human Brain Colouring Book* is a good example of this. You participate in the learning process: by colouring in you have to reflect on the information and make more connections to it; you will abstract your own thoughts and put them into action. Colour not only makes your information stand out, it makes it memorable.

Words

- Words should be BIGGER in the centre and smaller as the branches spread out.
- Use different SiZes to emphasize words.
- Only one word per branch; efficiency with words will make your mind maps easier to remember and give you freedom to be more creative as concepts are broken down and separated onto different branches.
  - *One word per branch will save space, allowing you to capture and consume more information.*
  - *Probably the most challenging part about constructing mind maps is condensing your thoughts down to single words: the temptation is to write short phrases or sentences across your branches. While this may be useful in pulling out quotes for presentations, you should practise using minimal words. This will also benefit you if you pull the words onto a memory network.*
- When reviewing your mind map you should practise seeing the key word and reciting the concepts, ideas and thoughts behind it.

Mirrors

- Nature – has an organic look and feel that attracts attention and engages in the information (it still has to be defined otherwise the map can become undecipherable, a common reason why mind maps can confuse).
- You – it reflects how we naturally think through imagination and association, mirroring the networks in our mind.
- A whole brain tool involving many cortical skills.

Use

Mind maps have two channels, taking in and putting out:

- Taking in
  - Capture the information (potentially rapidly).

- ▶ Anchor the information by colouring, decorating, adding in branches for your own thoughts and questions.
- ▶ Afterwards recreate your map to consolidate the information.
- ▶ Putting out
  - ▶ Alternate the content (branches, connectors and words) with the format (colours, images, codes and symbols).
  - ▶ Take regular breaks.

Insight

As a kid I think it is fair to say that I felt I was good at art. After leaving school and not drawing for ten years I seemed to lose the ability. When I first started mind mapping, I also had some beliefs about what people would think if my drawings looked childish. What I found was the opposite: people are usually intrigued when you mind map (especially in a meeting situation). Since I have been mind mapping for years now, the 'quality' of the maps has improved and I enjoy drawing again.

Action – Your mind map

Time limit: 15 minutes

Now recreate the mind map above using the style that feels right, adding in colour and any images that come to mind – it does not have to look like the mind map above but it should contain the same branches and words. Add at least two more branches, one that captures what you feel the benefits are, one that captures the challenges and any others that come to mind.

Insight

Do not be afraid of making mistakes. One thing I have noticed, especially when working with groups or individuals, is that people think it has to be perfect or as close as possible. The purpose is not to create a work of art, it is to either get something inside your head so you can use it or help to get something out of your head to solve problems, develop ideas or communicate messages. Our instinct can be that we are creating 'a picture' so we do not want to make mistakes; avoid falling into this trap. If it helps, buy a small whiteboard, where if something is not right, you can just rub it out and start again. I always have two spare branches on my mind maps to capture things that 'crop up' such as random thoughts and questions.

The four Cs

We have explored ideas behind mind mapping, how mind maps could work for you and how to mind map. The four Cs cover the main areas where mind mapping can be applied: create, capture, consume and communicate.

Although they are represented here as four separate entities, they most often cross over so that a mind map that starts for the purpose of capturing information in a meeting quickly becomes one that helps you consume and remember, communicate back what has been said and create new possibilities or solutions.

In the age of iPads and similar devices, software mind maps have made a big leap. They make it relatively quick to move your thoughts around, edit, add colour, link to documents or references on the internet and create a set of minutes or report on the outcomes of the meeting.

Paper and pen can still be quicker although there are disadvantages when capturing information: you generally don't have too much time to swap colours, although not a big drawback as afterwards you can add colour and imagery to create strong connections with information that is of importance.

Since you now understand 'how to mind map', there are a few subtleties to think about when putting them into practice.

Insight

My preference for capturing in meetings is a simple A5 whiteboard, with a coloured pen and an eraser. I remember when I had my first meeting with the new general manager taking over one of the departments at the BBC. iPads were very popular and this quickly became a topic of conversation; he even took a photograph. I later joked that he'd sent it round to Microsoft with the caption, 'This is how they do things at the Beeb.' This experience happened at pretty much every meeting I went to. The upshot is, you tend to be remembered.

CREATE

The benefits of mind mapping in the area of creation are many: whether it's a brainstorming new ideas session, solving a problem or creating a presentation, a mind map can help give you quality results.

State

Make sure you get yourself into a creative state. Think back to the chapter on creative memorization where we talked about sense memory and emotional recall.

▶ Think about your purpose and your ideal outcome.
▶ Use active daydreaming and draw words and pictures that represent this ideal outcome.

Questions

The questions you ask yourself and the self-talk that happens in your mind will direct and guide your output. In simple terms, ask a negative question, 'why can't I think of anything?' and your brain will go in search of an answer; at some point it will come back with one – you don't know enough, you're not creative, you're not good at this stuff.

Ask yourself a different question with the 'expectation' of getting an answer and you will get some useful feedback. What happens next? What would make the biggest difference? How can I make this work? Questions such as these asked in a curious and expectant way will create motivation and send your brain on a quest for knowledge. As you think up good questions to ask, add them to your mind map.

Overcoming blocks

At some point you will have a mental block or just need time to reflect, gather your thoughts and decide what happens next. When this happens, let yourself focus on the format of your map, creating imagery around certain areas of interest, colouring and doodling, using codes and symbols to highlight words or build relationships.

While you are in this state, you will notice that ideas will come to you for new content and connections with branches.

Alternate back and forth between the content of your map and the format; this will feed a rhythm that will allow you to progress with your ideas.

CAPTURE

In whatever career you are in, for most there will be occasions (sometimes frequent) when you have to capture notes, facts and actions, whether it is in meetings, presentations, conferences, seminars, lectures or classes.

What's relevant?

The key is to capture the information that is 'relevant': while this seems an obvious statement, it can be a challenge. Since you have to hone your thoughts down to single words, mind mapping conditions you in this art.

While listening and watching presentations, try to limit what you capture to information that you feel or think is connected to the purpose. Do not capture every little detail. If you are not sure, add a word to your question or thought branch that you can come back to later. This takes some practice; with enough repetition you will soon learn to 'filter' most of what is important.

Templates

Start with a template where possible, at minimum this is a central image (representing the topic), a branch for ideal outcomes, thoughts and questions and branches for any known agenda.

Time-sensitive

When capturing information there is less time to reflect, so you are relying on a clear purpose to guide you to what is relevant. Pragmatically you often won't have time to swap colours or draw lots of pictures, so if capturing at high speed, build the skeleton of your map that you can add to later to anchor the concepts and ideas in your mind.

CONSUME

Whereas capture is about identifying what is relevant, making connections and organizing, consuming is about understanding and remembering the information on your maps so you can put it into practice.

Mind maps 'map' perfectly to the learning cycle, taking information you have created or captured and making sense of it, through reflection, abstraction and some form of action. Comprehension starts when you are capturing and continues as you consume; depending on the complexity of the information you can allocate more time to this process, creating stronger connections with the information.

Input

With so much information to remember being passed around and the importance of keeping your knowledge (especially in your chosen field) up to date, it is useful if not imperative to have a way of consuming that information and having a reference for a later date.

You can make mind maps part of how you operate: as they are naturally more memorable than linear notes, they can be used to consume information from books, emails, documents and research in preparation for future meetings, presentations or interviews.

Used in conjunction with creative memorization, you have a powerful mental toolkit at your disposal.

Reflect

To understand the information you have captured, run through the map, reflecting on what it means. How does it relate to things you already know? What is this new information similar to? You are aiming to make some form of connection to help with your understanding. Metaphors are useful for this. Earlier we used the metaphor about the brain having over 100 billion neurons and compared that to the 100 billion trees in the rainforest; this was an easy picture to reflect on that gave an understanding to something which may have been completely new.

Abstract

When you have a difficult topic to grasp, abstracting your ideas helps you to take ownership. You then have to ask questions that will lead you towards a solution, in the same way as you would if you were creating a solution (which effectively you are). One of those solutions might be to ask someone for help or clarification. Abstracting is about taking what you have learned and putting it into your own words, making your own connections and points of reference to the information.

Actions

Decide what form of action you need to take if any: this may simply be storing the map for reference. If this is the case, you should start to build a classification for it or add it to one that already exists so it can be useful to you in the future. Perhaps you need it for a specific meeting or to gain knowledge that will help you perform more efficiently in your role.

The actions you take will be linked to your purpose: if you are mind mapping a presentation, you should rehearse using the mind map as a prompt, standing up and speaking aloud. If you are memorizing for an exam, you should test yourself by answering questions, initially using the mind map as a prompt and then without (mixed with creative memorization this becomes highly effective). If you have mapped notes from a meeting, simply play them back at the end of the meeting as a summary.

The actions you take complete the learning cycle and give you more sensory input to process, strengthening your connections to the information.

COMMUNICATE

Mind maps can be powerful tools for presentation and collaboration. Your aim should be to utilize the learning cycle in order to give your group or individual the best experience, to have them understand your message and give them something they can take away and use.

Groups

Because of the artistic and organic look and feel of a mind map, it naturally catches your attention. While looking at a mind map, it should tease curiosity within a group.

As with all presentations it is important that 'you' tell the story, the mind map is there as a visual reference that helps make your message more memorable. While you are giving a presentation, individuals will have their own stories and connections happening inside their heads; by focusing on specific parts of the mind map at the right time, the stories in their heads will become connected to your mind map.

Example

Imagine you are looking at a picture of the cortical skills of the brain on a mind map. I start talking about the time I was at school with a particular teacher who was quite strict (you may have had a teacher like this at your own school), wouldn't stand for any day dreaming nonsense and woe betide if you spoke out of turn, everything had to be written out neatly in black pen and this meant the children in that class were using primarily left-brain skills.

Chances are this may have triggered a memory of when you were at school. Since you are looking at the image of the cortical skills and you have experience of what that means, your experience gets associated with the picture on my mind map.

While or after the group reflect on their own experiences you should be challenging them to search for their own interpretations or solutions. This can be as simple as facilitating questions.

This should all build towards the group taking some form of action, making the information you have imparted to them useful to them in some way.

With a computer mind map presentation, you can capture their questions and thoughts live on the appropriate branch; if it's a large group, you may want someone to add these to the map while you continue to engage the audience.

One to one
If you are one-to-one with someone, mind maps are a subtle yet powerful tool. Without even actively saying anything, people will be drawn to the map, which you can use to reflect what has been said and build on ideas. It is therefore a great tool for helping to build rapport.

If you do mind map on a one-to-one basis, make sure you only capture the essential details. It is important to be connected to the person you are speaking to and use the map sparingly.

If you get the balance right, one-to-ones are a great opportunity to have some real collaboration and engage some physicality in the creation of the mind map. Depending on your level of rapport, you can ask the person you are working with to add branches and draw pictures to explain what they mean, then reflect and summarize that back to them.

The mind map becomes a shared experience.

In practice

We have only scratched the surface of mind mapping and there is a lot more underneath; ultimately it is about finding your own style and putting it into practice.

Action – Where in your life?

Time limit: 15 minutes
Think of all the different areas in your life where you could apply mind mapping. Create a mind map with these branches as a minimum:

- ▶ Create
- ▶ Capture
- ▶ Consume
- ▶ Communicate
- ▶ Thoughts
- ▶ Questions

On each branch connect areas of your life where you could put these skills into practice.

KEYS TO A GREAT MEMORY

▶ Mind maps are tools for creating, capturing, consuming and communicating.

▶ Mind maps mirror the way we think, reflecting the internal connections in your mind.

▶ Identify the level of cortical skills you use in your current note-taking; compare this with how many you use when mind mapping or when using visual notes.

▶ Find your style – think about what you can do to make mind maps work for you.

▶ Regularly practise mind mapping following the *How to mind map* guidelines, using branches, images, colours and words.

▶ Create with your mind maps by getting in the right state, using the power of questions to guide you and overcoming blocks by alternating format and content.

▶ Capture effectively with your mind maps by priming yourself for relevant information, setting up templates and being pragmatic about what you can achieve in the time you have.

▶ Consume rapidly through incorporating an abundance of sensory input, using your map as a mirror to reflect on what you know, abstracting and capturing your own thoughts and questions and using your map as a tool to take some form of action.

▶ Communicate dynamically with groups using your mind map to raise curiosity and 'tell the story'. Engage deeply on a one-to-one level in a subtle and rapport-building way that evokes collaboration.

▶ Mind maps can be used for facilitating ideas, problem solving, increasing comprehension, improving memory retention, rapid note taking, engaging presentations and more.

9

Reading strategies: Double or triple your speed

In this chapter you will learn:
- *how to measure your current reading speed*
- *benefits of creating purpose and direction*
- *how to capture the 10,000-foot view*
- *how to double your reading speed with speed reading.*

There are many books that go into great detail on reading strategies. The purpose of this section is to give you practical techniques you can start using today that will speed up consumption and comprehension of reading material.

Benchmark

If you want to increase your reading speed, it is a valuable use of time to benchmark yourself so you can measure your success as your speed increases. This will also help create beliefs to back up your progress and let you identify which areas you need to improve in.

Action – Benchmark your speed

Time limit: 5 minutes
Before beginning, choose a book that is of interest to you and find yourself a stopwatch.

- ▶ Note where you begin and, when you are ready, start reading.
- ▶ After one minute, stop reading and make a note of where you got to.

> ▶ Count the number of **lines** you have read in total and make a note.
> ▶ Count the number of **words** in three lines and divide by 3 (this gives an average).
> ▶ Average **number of words x number of lines** = words per minute (**wpm**).
>
> If there is an average of 12 words per line and you have read 50 lines, that would give you a benchmark reading speed of 600 wpm.

Purpose and direction

When you think back to books or documents you have read in the past, how much attention have you paid before you start reading to your ultimate purpose? Do you generally have a good idea of what you are looking for? Are you priming yourself for information that is relevant?

As we have previously seen, priming is an important aspect of setting ourselves up to remember. By having a strong purpose and direction about why this information is important and what you think is relevant inside this book or document, you set your brain's radar to be on the lookout.

> ### Action – Finding purpose and direction
>
> **Time limit: 3 minutes**
> ▶ Think of a problem or challenge that needs to be solved.
> ▶ What do you gain by solving it; what is your purpose?
> ▶ Choose a factual book that you think has some information that could help.
> ▶ Reaffirm your purpose.
> ▶ By simply reading the table of contents, identify whether this book is relevant. If it isn't, move on.
> ▶ What level of detail do you need to understand?
> ▶ How much time do you think you will need to commit?

Example

▶ *Imagine you are a manager and have a problem with team performance.*

- ▶ *Your purpose is to find some way to identify the issues and improve team performance (your purpose is now clear – you are primed).*
- ▶ *You go in search of books that could help and select Ken Blanchard's One Minute Manager book about building high performing teams.*
- ▶ *You reaffirm your purpose.*
- ▶ *You scan the index and identify anything that looks relevant, e.g. techniques you could put into practice straight away and measure against current performance. This book has things that look relevant so you continue.*
- ▶ *The level of detail you need will be high around the one or two techniques you identify and can be less for the rest of the book.*
- ▶ *Taking the size of the book into account, you could estimate that within two hours you will have identified what you need and have understood it to a level where you could put it into practice and test it out.*

10,000-foot view

Once your purpose has been established, you can use previewing as a technique to set up the mental scaffolding to give you the 10,000-foot view. Previewing should be a fairly short phase lasting no longer than two to five minutes: explore and seek out parts of the book that catch your attention in line with your purpose. Reflect on parts of the book that are familiar to you and dive briefly into any sections that have new information. There is no need to stop for more than three to five seconds.

You may find that something is so interesting that you just start reading: avoid this trap; the main objective for previewing is to build up a big picture view and identify some nuggets of interest.

After previewing, it is useful to consolidate your thoughts, running the learning cycle, reflecting, abstracting and creating some new actions. If mind maps are working for you, it is a great opportunity to put them into practice. Without going back to the book for any more detail, you simply start mind mapping what you can remember from your preview. You will be tempted to look at the book for details: avoid this and just create a branch that captures questions you have or things you can't quite remember but want to dig into in more detail. Add a branch that communicates how you would put some of the information into practice. While reflecting on the mind map as a whole you can also clarify your purpose.

> ### Action – Preview time
>
> **Time limit: 10 minutes**
> ▶ Find a book of your choice and spend no longer than five minutes previewing and five minutes mind mapping your thoughts.

Double your speed

Speed reading strategies deal with some common reading problems, e.g. back-skipping, when you read a sentence and then unconsciously skip back to read it again, and regression, when you go back to words, phrases or sentences you didn't understand or think you need to clarify.

The following strategies offer the opportunity to at least double your current reading speed.

GUIDING

As children you would have been taught to read by using your finger, guiding your eye across the page. When reading, your eye moves in fixations, rather than a smooth movement: it will jump across points in a sentence. Someone practised in speed reading will take larger jumps, pause for less time at each jump, avoid jumping backwards and take in more words with each jump. The outcome of this is that reading speed is increased and comprehension is increased as more words are taken in together.

> ### Action – Chopsticks!
>
> **Time limit: 5 minutes**
> Continue with the book you chose for the first 'Action' of this chapter and get your stopwatch ready. Find yourself a pen or some type of pointer; a chopstick works very well. Use your chopstick as a guide, in the same way you used your finger as a child; move the chopstick underneath the sentence, let your eyes take in groups of words at a time. As you move the chopstick smoothly from line to line, do not back-skip or regress to things you have previously read.

For this test, move the pointer slightly faster than is comfortable.

▶ Note where you begin and, when you are ready, start reading.
▶ After one minute stop reading and make a note of where you got to.
▶ Count the number of lines you have read in total and make a note.
▶ Count the number of words in three lines and divide by 3 to give you an average.
▶ Average number of words x number of lines = words per minute (wpm).
▶ Compare this wpm with your previous wpm.

PERIPHERAL

This is a technique that is referred to in Ron Davis's *The Gift of Dyslexia* that focuses on the mind's eye – 'a mental perception point at which a person looks at mental images or thoughts'. The mind's eye is mentioned in various reading books, yoga classes and martial arts; this is so you become more aware of the world around you – in martial arts this makes you more effective when blocking attacks.

Action – Engage your peripheral

Time limit: 2 minutes

By engaging your peripheral vision, your scope of vision widens and also deepens. There are several ways to practise this that have been referred to in many books. A good one is in Paul Scheele's *Photoreading*, where he refers to this as the 'tangerine technique', although it could be any object you wish, a tennis ball or any small object.

▶ Imagine that there is a tennis ball or tangerine in front of you; see it in every detail (think back to the sense memory exercise).
▶ Now reach forward and pick it up; examine it.
▶ Now place it at the back of your head (on top of your crown).
▶ As you let go, become aware that it is still there.
▶ As you focus on it, notice that it drifts back about 15 cms (6 inches), upwards at 45 degrees.
▶ Imagine that you are now 'seeing from this point' – your mind's eye.
▶ See the page in front of you from this point.

This will feel strange to begin with and take some practice, but you should notice your field of vision opening up.

SUBVOCALIZATION

Part of the objective of speed reading is not to subvocalize, i.e. say every word in your head while reading. Having said that, it can be very effective to vocalize particular words that spring out and catch your attention: these tend to be the ones that are of most relevance.

Action – Silent reading

Time limit: 5 minutes
Bring the last few 'Actions' together. Use a pointer, find your mind's eye and read the next section without subvocalizing. Again, move the pointer faster than is comfortable

- ▶ Note where you begin and, when you are ready, start reading.
- ▶ After one minute stop reading and make a note of where you got to.
- ▶ Count the number of lines you have read in total and make a note.
- ▶ Count the number of words in three lines and divide by 3 to give you an average.
- ▶ Average number of words x number of lines = words per minute (wpm).
- ▶ Compare this wpm with your previous wpm.

BELIEVE YOU CAN

Belief can have a big impact on performance, whether it is a belief about what we can remember, how good we are at sports or how fast we can read. By imagining yourself going faster or performing better than you thought was possible, you create positive references that support beliefs about what is possible.

Action – How far can you go?

Time limit: 5 minutes
- ▶ Stand up straight and, keeping your feet still throughout, raise your right arm directly in front of you, pointing your finger straight ahead.

> ▶ Now, moving around to your right, go as far as you can and note where your finger is pointing.
> ▶ Bring your arm back to resting.

Now we condition a belief.

> ▶ Imagine that you are standing up as you were before, right arm raised directly in front of you, pointing your finger straight ahead.
> ▶ Imagine moving around to your right, but this time you notice that you go much further than you did before and the movement seems effortless; notice how this feels; see how much further you have gone than you did previously.
> ▶ Open your eyes, stand up, raise your right arm directly in front of you and go as far as you can round to the right.

After doing this, a large number of people will go at least six inches further than they did the first time. You can use this same technique with reading. Imagine yourself reading faster than you ever have before, effortlessly gliding across sentences, capturing whole sentences at a time, instantly making sense of everything you read. If you make this real enough in your mind, your brain will start creating references that this is possible.

Action – Speed reading in action

Time limit: 5 minutes
Bring together all the reading strategies in this section. Spend the first two minutes imagining yourself reading faster than ever before, set your mind's eye, get your pointer ready, only subvocalize essential words and push yourself faster than before, gliding your pointer across the page, taking in groups of words with each jump.

> ▶ Note where you begin and, when you are ready, start reading.
> ▶ After one minute stop reading and make a note of where you got to.
> ▶ Count the number of lines you have read in total and make a note.

- ▶ Count the number of words in three lines and divide by 3 to give you an average.
- ▶ Average number of words x number of lines = words per minute (wpm).
- ▶ Compare this wpm with your previous wpm.

In practice

Like all other strategies in this book, effective speed reading doesn't happen overnight. The good news is, these reading strategies are easy to practise, as you are most likely reading something everyday.

TEN-DAY CHALLENGE

Take up the ten-day challenge! Each time you read over the next ten days put some or all of these techniques into practice and check your wpm at the end to measure your improvement.

KEYS TO A GREAT MEMORY

▶ Find your benchmark so you can track your improvement and increase your motivation.

▶ Turn on your mental radar by defining your purpose and set yourself up to track down the relevant information.

▶ Use rapid previewing to build up the 10,000-foot view and identify some of the key nuggets of information.

▶ At least double your current speed by employing speed reading in your day-to-day life.

▶ Get out your chopsticks and overcome back-skipping and regression with guiding techniques.

▶ Engage your peripheral vision by seeing from your mind's eye; use the tangerine technique to get started.

▶ Practise silent reading and only subvocalizing relevant words, increasing your speed and comprehension.

▶ Spend time imagining reading at high speed to create solid references in your mind and powerful beliefs that increase your speed.

Part 3
How to remember

'Repetition is the mother of skill.'

Anthony Robbins

10

Lifestyle: Master your memory

In this chapter you will learn:
- *how to experience the value of immersion*
- *how to get organized with your 'things to do'*
- *how to create your mindset for remembering names*
- *how to tap into your natural memory for directions.*

Immersion

When put into practice, creative memorization can be a powerful skill in the context of your everyday life. To become skilful at anything you have to use repetition; through repetition you will strengthen your neuronal pathways for that specific skill. Through immersion, actually living with these skills, you work towards mastery and the possibility of creating real change.

The concepts of creative memorization, mind mapping and speed reading can be grasped relatively quickly, but making them part of 'how you think' and putting them into practice so that you gain real value without it being a 'chore', in the beginning at least, can be a challenge.

Like any new skill, you may hit a bump in the road, there might be a temptation to fall back into old habits that are less effective and take what initially feels like the easy route. By immersing yourself in the following techniques, you can cruise over those bumps.

Insight

During the game show I created, *Memory Masters*, I ran a two-day seminar with 30 contestants. They then had two weeks to remember a large amount of information. Rather than just running the seminar, then leaving them to create memory networks and reference stories of their own, I would help by breaking down the information into reference stories to give them a 'kick-start', as it were. This meant that by the end of those two weeks their brains were truly immersed in creating these types of pattern, and by the second week, most contestants were substituting my images for their own, which was the goal.

Things to do

It is a short and simple place to start. You already have the skills to remember the things that you need to do. The value comes from asking yourself, 'How can memorizing specific things to do save me time and make me more organized?' Perhaps there are details about upcoming meetings that are useful to be able to call on, maybe there times when you need to remember things to do from ad hoc conversations, it could be that it is simply a quick way of keeping your skills up to scratch.

Insight

I don't memorize 'everything' I need to do; I tend to focus on tasks that have a higher priority, that are important enough to spend a few minutes putting them onto a memory network. I will usually start the day by memorizing key meetings and tasks; since I'm on the move a lot, it creates a sense of control to always know what is coming up next and how one conversation may relate to another conversation happening later that day.

Action – What are your reasons?

Time limit: 3 minutes
- ▶ What are your reasons for creating 'things to do' memory networks?
- ▶ How would you use them in your life?

Once you have compelling reasons for creating your 'things to do' networks, work out how many memory networks you need by classifying them by purpose.

Examples

- ▶ *Family*
- ▶ *Business*

▶ *Daily*
▶ *Events*
▶ *Ad hoc*

You may choose to create a mind map or other system that captures all of your 'things to do' as well as keeping them on your memory networks.

Action – 'Things to do' networks

Time limit: 5 minutes
  ▶ Choose three categories that make sense for you and create three separate memory networks with ten nodes in each.

'Things to do' is an easy way to build up your mental muscles and get yourself in shape for some of the more heavyweight memorizing.

Names

Whether in social situations or in business, the ability to remember people's names is something that not only makes a person stand out and be remembered, but also offers opportunities to create rapport and build relationships. Everyone likes it when you remember their name; it is one of the simplest things you can do to demonstrate that you have an interest in that person.

Unfortunately, not remembering a name is something that can create many awkward situations. You will no doubt have met people who announce that they are so bad at remembering names they won't even try.

Creative memorization presents a process for remembering a person's name that will vastly increase your chances of 'getting it right'. It is unlikely that you will remember everyone you meet; there will be times when the connections you have made were not strong enough or they have simply faded away. One day you may remember 30 people in a room, but if you meet them one month later the connections you made have faded. The strength of the connection will depend on many factors, one of the most relevant being 'How important is it that you remember this person?'

Insight

I usually start my seminars by memorizing everyone's name, but I don't
initially draw attention to it. I meet everyone individually and introduce
myself, then after the first 20–30 minutes or so, I start directing thoughts or
questions to people in the session using their name. After a short time there
is always a small buzz going around the room – 'He knows all our names!'
I have tried many variations on memorizing names and so far I have found
the strategies I am about to teach you work best. From talking to memory
athletes around the world, I know that everyone will have their own 'take' on
it. Once you have a solid framework, I would suggest playing with this to find
a way that works for you.

MINDSET

You will no doubt have noticed that a pattern is emerging around
priming yourself to remember. Memorizing names is slightly different
from other kinds of memorizing as you do not tend to have time to
prepare, in the same way you could prepare for, let's say, an exam.
However, there are ways that you can set yourself up for names; it all
comes down to creating the right mindset.

Meeting new people is often unexpected, so remembering their name
is sometimes the last thing on your mind. Sometimes the reason you
are meeting seems more important than the people you are meeting. In
either case it's not so much remembering who they are, as not getting
their name to begin with. Sometimes you meet a large group of people
all at once and believe there is no way you will remember everyone's
name so there doesn't seem any point in trying, and even if you do try,
you get the first three or four and then forget them within seconds.

To deal with these challenges you need to construct a specific mindset
to remember names and condition it until it becomes instinctive. The
correct mindset involves running through a set of steps every time
you meet someone; with repetition, the right neuronal networks will
fire up instinctively. Make remembering people's names your prime
goal; put it right at the top of your list.

Action – Condition yourself to remember

Time limit: 5 minutes
Spend time over the next seven days going through this quick
action or your own variation of it. Try it now.

- As you sit down, become aware of your body in the chair; as your muscles relax, let go of all tension. Focus on your feet and bring your attention up through your calf muscles, past your knees and into your thighs; notice how your legs are relaxing. Enjoy this feeling as it travels up through your hips, waist and into your chest. Become aware of the muscles in your chest and let that awareness drift into your shoulders and down your arms all the way to your fingertips. Let that awareness come back up to your neck and all around your face and head; notice how relaxed you are as you sit in the chair.
- Now spend a few minutes thinking about the people you might meet today. Are there people you meet regularly you still don't know yet? What could you do to remember their names? As you think about meeting these people, imagine getting yourself ready to remember them, feel confident that you will find it easy to remember their names and use them naturally in conversation. See yourself in conversation with people throughout the day, remembering their names and notice how they remember yours. Notice that before you meet people, you are already priming yourself to remember their name; you are interested to see how quickly you can memorize it and how long you can retain it. Realize how easy this is and how good it makes you feel.
- Spend a few minutes rehearsing meeting people throughout the day and remembering their names effortlessly.
- When you have finished, take some deep breaths and feel a relaxing energy coming into your body, setting you up for the day.

Insight

If all you did were conditioning yourself to remember names, you would notice a big improvement. You can also download a full-length version of this conditioning session from http://www.howtorememberanything.co.uk.

ATTENTION

Be aware of **where** you met someone as well as **why** you met them. If you can remember the location at a later time, this can help you to remember details about the episode, including their name.

While you are working through the process of conditioning, as soon as you meet a person (even someone you know well), pay attention to how they look. This may feel strange at first and you have to find the balance between paying attention and staring.

Pay attention to the overall look, the shape of their head, shape and colour of eyes, what their ears remind you of, how they move their mouth, whether they have a Roman nose or a large forehead or perhaps they lead with their chin. Study their features and bring that together with their hair, skin colour and type; is it smooth, rough, freckly, etc.? Looking at them as a whole, do they remind you of any kind of animal or famous person that would help you remember them?

Insight

Remembering back to when I used to condition myself to remember names, I would sit on the train and start noticing how people looked. As an actor I was always pretty used to 'people watching'. As someone who is practising remembering names, it is about finding the differences in how people look and playing with those differences in your mind. Luckily, people on London's tube don't tend to pay too much attention.

FEATURES

While you are studying a person's face, become aware of their most prominent features and mentally exaggerate them. Create a clear mental image of that person in your mind. Their face will effectively become the 'node' or 'location' that you connect their name to.

Action – Exaggerate me!

Time limit: 5 minutes
Get a picture of someone you know well (perhaps go to Facebook or Flickr if you use any of those sites for uploading photographs) and spend five minutes studying people's features and exaggerating them.

LISTEN

There can be embarrassment associated with not hearing a person's name to begin with; sometimes that is through lack of attention and other times it is simply because the person you are speaking to has a name you have never heard before. If you have the right mindset, you should be primed to listen; if you are listening, then you should catch their name in the first place. In the situation where you can't hear the person's name clearly or it is difficult to pronounce, simply ask them to repeat their name or spell it; if you say this out of interest in them, people generally don't mind.

When you hear their name, repeat it back to them out loud: this will make stronger connections with the name and the person. There will be some situations where this may seem awkward; being introduced to a group of people could be one of them. In this case, there are two things you can do:

▶ Take a chance and memorize their names as quickly as you can: by doing this you should pick up the majority of them. Use people's names early in conversation; if there is one you can't remember, simply ask them again.

▶ Listen to names being said once and then say to the group as a whole, 'I just want to make sure I have everybody's name', and start running through each one out loud. People will realize if you haven't got it first time round and will tell you their name again. The first method is probably preferable, but if you pull this one off it can be very impressive and you will no doubt be remembered too.

CONNECTION

Almost in parallel with listening to the name, you need to be creating an image for their name, either a sound-image or a natural-image, and making a connection with the feature you have identified. This is probably the most challenging aspect of remembering names, but it is also the part that will enable you to remember 20–50 people in the room.

You will find that with practice, as with numbers, you will start to build up a vocabulary of images to represent names, so if a name is familiar to you, it will be a simple task to create a connection. The challenge happens when you are faced with a name you have never heard before or rarely hear. In these cases you can usually create an image for the first syllable of the name and through using the name in conversation create a strong association with the person. Afterwards you can reinforce the image for when you meet someone with the same name in the future.

Example

If you meet a person called John, there are several images that spring to mind – a john (toilet) or maybe you know someone called John who likes to paint. You could use a paintbrush or a toilet. If John has a prominent forehead, you might imagine him painting it with your favourite colour.

It is always best never to let people know the images you are creating in your mind. Once you get to know the person you won't need to refer to the images, as you will just 'know' their name.

If John's second name was Cartwright, you might imagine him painting his forehead with your favourite colour while lying in a cart – this would all be happening right in front of you.

Action – Remember my name

Time limit: 10 minutes
Using the strategies for names, memorize as many names as you can in 10 minutes.

Alison Shepherd

John Norris

Joseph Pitcher

Carol Williams

Nick Brownlow

Cola Richmond

Caroline Marsden

Emmalene Evans

John Norris

Figure 10.1a Memorizing names.

Action – Name recall

Time limit: 5 minutes

Write down as many people as you can remember.

Figure 10.1b Recalling names.

If you find you can't immediately recall a name you memorized, ask yourself the question 'What is their name?' and mentally repeat 'Their name will come to me shortly'. As you say this, expect to get an answer. We have all had the experience of seeing someone in the street and you know you know them but the name doesn't come, only for two days later the name to jump back into your head, 'It's John!'

Don't be afraid to fail, play with these techniques and spend some time getting them wrong. As you start to hone your own style, you will notice that the number of names you remember increases.

To remember someone for a longer period of time, find out more details about them; the more you know, the more connections you will make and the easier their name will be to remember.

BUILDING YOUR NETWORK

It is questionable in this day and age whether there is value in memorizing the list of contacts contained in your phone or computer or diary.

While impressive, the need may be minimal, with most data backed up on your computer and maybe in the 'cloud'.

In a career sense, however, there can be major benefits and value in knowing people in your network and key facts about them. With social networks such as Twitter, Facebook and LinkedIn, the ability to build that network is easier than it has ever been. The old saying 'It's not what you know but who you know', rings true in a lot of cases; if you have the knowledge and you know the right people, you set yourself up to have a good chance of succeeding in the things you aim to achieve.

As well as building up your personal network, if you are in a career that requires managing a group of stakeholders, it is not only essential that you remember their names, it is beneficial to remember details about what drives them and what their priorities and needs are. Having that information on tap will let you react quickly to situations.

Action – Mapping your network

Time limit: 10 minutes
Think about who is in your personal or stakeholder network (you may want to do both).

▶ Create a mind map that puts them into different social groups that could potentially influence your career (employers, employees, partners, opportunities, etc.). If you use something such as Google+, the 'Circles' feature can be very powerful, allowing you to create subsets of your larger circles.

▶ If you manage a group of stakeholders and you are mapping them out, you may want to group them into relevant business areas (product, design, finance, marketing, sales, or whatever structure works for your business).

▶ For each person in your network, what do you know about them? Is there anything that you could offer them that would benefit them? Is there any way that working with someone could be mutually beneficial? Who might be able to utilize your talents?

If you are familiar with the power (the amount of resources a person can bring to a situation) vs interest (their level of commitment) graph, you can use creative memorization to construct a memory network for each quadrant and mentally group the people you need to manage.

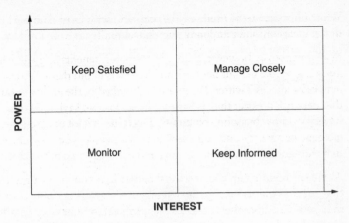

Figure 10.2 Power vs interest graph.

If you have 20 stakeholders, you may have five in each quadrant, for example. If a stakeholder has high power and high interest, they will go in the quadrant that says 'manage closely'. If a person moves, you simply mentally shift them to a different location.

Over time you can build up a set of memory networks that help you store specific information about all of your clients, creating reference stories for their specific challenges and objectives. This is something that can add value to the notes you keep.

Directions

With the huge number of satellite navigation systems available and mapping devices on smart phones, the need to remember directions seems less and less important. There is still an interest in being able to master this skill, though, and potentially it could be essential to your career, if you are planning to become a cab driver, for example, and have to memorize 'The Knowledge'.

Insight

One of the games in *Memory Masters* was to memorize a large section of 'The Knowledge'; these are the routes London cab drivers have to learn in order to qualify as a driver. Tests have shown that cab drivers have an enlarged hippocampus, the part of the brain that is known to help form episodic memories and is used for spatial memory.

To remember directions there are two useful steps: prime yourself with the information beforehand and then actually take the journey. With the current technology available in the form of Google Maps streetview, it can be a relatively simple process to memorize the journey beforehand.

Action – Holborn to Regent's Park

Time limit: 15 minutes
The following directions are from the AA Routeplanner.

To begin with we will create some codes to represent common words:

- Right – rat
- Left – leaves
- Forward – headbutt

These are examples you can refer to, but where possible try to create your own.

From Holborn–Strand–Covent Garden, London **to** Regent's Park, London

Distance: 2.6 miles Time: 0 hr 12 min

Directions	Reference story	Active testing (out loud)
Start out on Drury Lane, Central London		
Turn right onto Kemble Street	**Kimble** Shanks eating a **Rat**	Drury Lane, turn right onto Kemble Street
Turn left onto the A4200	**RaiNing(42) SauCe(00)** and **Leaves**	Left, A4200
At Holborn Underground Station continue forward onto Southampton Row – A4200	**Headbutt South Ham**	Forward onto Southampton Row

Directions	Reference story	Active testing (out loud)
At traffic signals turn left onto the A501 Signposted Ring Road		
	Leaves making a **RING**	Left, Ring Road
At Euston Underpass continue forward onto the A501 Signposted Ring Road, Marylebone		
	Headbutt Mary	Forward, Marylebone
At Great Portland Street Underground Station turn left onto Osnaburgh Street – A4201	**Leaves** falling on **Ice Berg**	Left, Osnaburgh Street
At next traffic signals turn right onto the A4201	**RatRiNSeD** dry	Right, A4201
Take right hand lane and continue forward onto Albany Street - A4201	**Headbutt Ale Bee**	Forward, Albany
Turn left onto Chester Gate	**Leaves** on **Gate**	Left, Chester Gate
Turn right onto Outer Circle	**Rats** outside a **Circle**	Right, Outer Circle
Turn left onto Chester Road	**Leaves** on **Chest**	Left, Chester
Turn right onto Inner Circle	**Rat** inside a **Circle**	Right, Inner Circle
Arrive on Inner Circle		

Source: AA Route Planner © 2006-201_ TomTom. All rights reserved. This material is proprietary and the subject of copyright protection, database right protection and other intellectual property rights owned by TomTom or its suppliers. The use of this material is subject to the terms of a license agreement. Any unauthorized copying or disclosure of this material will lead to criminal and civil liabilities.

Now that you have primed yourself with the information, you need to associate the reference stories with a memory network. To do this you can use the 'actual locations' found on Google Maps streetview.

The locations will become your memory nodes – Drury Lane, Holborn Station, Euston Underpass, etc.

Example

You go to Google Maps streetview, find the intersection of Drury Lane and Kimble Street, pick a specific point (perhaps the restaurant on the corner) and imagine Kimble Shanks eating a Rat. Continue by associating each one of your reference stories with appropriate locations along the route.

If you don't have access to the internet, you can create your own memory network with 12 nodes (one for each reference story). When you take the journey, simply refer to the stories on your memory network.

If you happen to be learning 'The Knowledge', this is a great way of priming yourself before driving a route and consolidating the information afterwards. It also makes it easy to memorize points of interest along the route, as your route is effectively a memory network.

Physicality

Creative memorization can play a part in learning a new physical skill, be it a sport, dance routine or even cooking. When learning a physical skill, creative memorization can set up 'markers' or 'visual cues' on your physical journey. These visual cues let you know where you should be at a particular time.

You may be learning to play golf, so you use the chain method to create a set of visual cues that remind you of the grip, stance, backswing, downswing and follow-through. Then by recreating the swing in your mind, you begin to construct a memory of a good golf swing.

Insight

Having been an actor and dancer in a number of London West End shows and on tour, I have had first-hand experience in the application of creative memorization in dance. When I was playing Cosmo in *Singin' in the Rain*, the choreographer Stephen Mear had a vision of what one of the numbers, 'Make 'em Laugh', should be. Rather than working in a strict manner where you memorized the steps, then moved on, he was collaborative to the point where he allowed me to throw out some ideas. In effect he was encouraging the learning cycle. He was able to guide this process until he achieved the results he was looking for. To add to this, in rehearsals I was able to 'imagine' visual cues that triggered the next sequence, this was only needed until I became completely familiar with the routine and it felt like second nature.

As well as creating visual cues, thinking about the learning cycle while learning a new physical activity will help in how quickly you pick it up. Find what is similar in this new skill to others you have practised in the past. Play with your own ideas and experiment through trial, error and repetition, honing and adapting as you go.

For anything that requires remembering physical movements, you are generally dealing with procedural memories, relying on what you unconsciously know and building on this. If, for example, you are a martial artist in wing chun and someone shows you a unique combination of moves that are made up of techniques you have previously learned, you will find it easier to remember than someone who has never done wing chun but has practised karate for a number of years.

Rehearsal is key in any physical activity you are involved in, not just going through the movements but getting every fibre of your being involved; by this very essence you are creating a multitude of memorable connections.

KEYS TO A GREAT MEMORY

▶ Repetition is the mother of skill: immerse yourself in creative memorization to take you on the road to mastery.

▶ Gently build up your memory muscles, classifying your 'things to do' and creating a structure to get things done.

▶ Make remembering names part of your day-to-day mindset; condition yourself to remember names for the next seven days.

▶ Pay attention to the details: remember where and why as well as the person's overall look.

▶ Use creative memorization and make names through exaggeration, listening and connection.

▶ Build a network of people that will be mutually beneficial and practise your skills by remembering key information.

▶ If you manage stakeholders, capture them on a mind map and memorize them depending on their level of power vs interest.

▶ Use creative memorization to memorize directions quickly with the aid of Google Maps.

▶ Take advantage of visual cues in learning physical skills such as dance, sport and cooking.

11

General knowledge: Sowing the seeds of knowledge

In this chapter you will learn:
- *how to prime yourself for knowledge*
- *how to remember facts and figures*
- *how to make complex information easy to remember*
- *how to remember and cook your favourite recipes.*

The ability to reel off general knowledge in itself can be very impressive. By exploring how to memorize different types of factual information, you allow your brain to immerse itself in the practice of creative memorization, working towards a point where it becomes second nature.

With this chapter you should initially read through it to get a sense of what it entails, then work through the 'Actions' that you feel you will get the most value from, using it as a resource you can come back to again and again.

Sowing the seeds

By taking time to remember general knowledge, you are effectively sowing the seeds that will set you up for similar knowledge in the future. If, for example, you know that Ryan Lochte set a world record at the 2011 World Swimming Championships for the 200 metres individual medley with a time of 1:54.00, when you watch the 2012 Olympics you will have a point of reference and an opportunity to connect more information if you choose to do so. The simple fact of knowing the time to beat can also change your emotional engagement with any events which Ryan Lochte and his famous arch-rival Michael Phelps participate in. Since you are primed you will 'notice' more stories about their rivalry than you might have otherwise. By having an emotional engagement and being primed in this way, your brain will naturally be directing your attention to remember more and the information becomes relevant and interesting. The ideas that you have sown here grow as you naturally make more connections.

For most of the 'Actions' you will go through in this chapter, you will need to create memory networks to store the information. It is recommended that you spend some time brainstorming events in your life from which you can construct memory networks. Alternatively, a quick and easy way (as mentioned previously) is to use Google Maps to construct your memory networks. In some cases there will be a more natural memory network to store the information, as with oceans.

> **Insight**
>
> While going through the 'Actions' in this chapter, reflect on any similarities there are between the information you have to learn in your current role. Think of the best ways you could structure your own information and how you could utilize these same types of strategy.

Geography

Geography is a complex and wide-ranging topic. For the purposes of putting creative memorization into practice we will look at a simple and very small slice that demonstrates how to remember some facts in relation to oceans and mountains of the world.

Action – Oceans and mountains

Time limit: 20 minutes

- Rather than creating an unrelated memory network for the oceans, a more natural method is simply to get a globe and in the Pacific create your reference story, using your natural spatial memory to 'see' where the Pacific is.
- With mountains you may want initially to create a memory network as a point of reference until you just 'know' where they are.

▶ For each example, create the images clearly in your mind and associate to your memory node.

Example

Pacific is the memory node – imagine Mariana eating a Meal that is Funky in the middle of the Pacific. Make it real and dial up the intensity, recite aloud 'Pacific – Deepest point – Mariana Trench 35,827 ft.'

Oceans – deepest point	Reference story (examples)
Pacific – Mariana Trench – 35,827 ft	**Mariana** eating a **MeaL**(35) that is **FuNKy**(827)
Atlantic – Puerto Rico Trench – 30,246 ft	**Sharks** (West Side Story) fighting hol**MeS**(30) with e**NeRGy**(246)
Indian – Java Trench – 24,460 ft	Cup of **Java** drunk by he**NRy**(24) with **RoaCHeS**(460)
Southern – Southern Ocean – 23,737 ft	The Southerner **NeMoy**(23) reading a **CoMiC**(737)
Arctic – Arctic Basin – 18,456 ft	Basin with a **DoVe**(18) in **ReLiSH**(456)

For mountains we will create a code for the various countries:

▶ Nepal/Tibet – NuT
▶ Pakistan/China – PaC
▶ India/Nepal – IaN

You might imagine yourself on the top of **Everest** with only **NuTs** around your neck. While having a **NaP**(29), **SNooPy**(029) licks your face.

Mountains (all Himalayas – except K2)	Reference story (your stories)
Everest – Nepal/Tibet – 29,029ft	
K2 – Karakoram – Pakistan/China – 28,251ft	
Kanchenjunga – India/Nepal – 28,169 ft	

Mountains (all Himalayas – except K2)	Reference story (your stories)
Lhotse – Nepal/Tibet – 27,940 ft	
Makalu – Nepal/Tibet – 27,838 ft	
Cho Oyu – Nepal/Tibet – 26,864 ft	
Dhaulagiri – Nepal – 26,795 ft	
Manaslu – Nepal – 26,781ft	
Nanga Parbat – Pakistan – 26,660 ft	
Annapurna – Nepal – 26,545 ft	

Entertainment

The next 'Action' is specifically designed to test your mental stamina, remembering every single best picture Oscar winner dating back to 1927–8.

Action – Oscar winners, Best Picture

Time limit: 30 minutes (examples)
There are several methods of memorizing Best Picture Oscar winners. You could associate the name of the movie with the year on its own without using a memory network or associate the movie with the year and then connect to a memory network node:

Memory node: Chair, Movie – Date: 1927–8, *Wings*

A *NaVy* Seal with *Wings* sitting on your *Chair*

Or since the data is in chronological order you could construct a memory network in such a way that it is easy to find a particular number by chunking up your nodes (refer to *How to memorize a memory network* in the 'Action' box in Chapter 6).

Chunk of 6: → 28, 29, 30, 31, 32, 33 *(these are the non-calendar years 27/28, etc.)*

Chunk of 7: → 34, 35, 36, 37, 38, 39, 40 *(by taking your second chunk up to 40 the years following this will be easier to remember)*

Chunk of 5: → 41, 42, 43, 44, 45 *(continue with chunks of 5)*

You know that your first node (Chair) is number 27/28 – the chair has Wings.

Using this approach, you would only need to associate the name of the movie to your node, rather than the movie and the year. You will have to spend more time learning where the numbers are.

I have given examples using the first approach back to 1971 (the year I was born).

Oscar winners	Reference story (examples)
2010 – *The King's Speech*	The King with a DaZzling(10) Crown
2009 – *The Hurt Locker*	Rubbing SoaP(09) on The Hurt Locker
2008 – *Slumdog Millionaire*	Actor from Slumdog breaking into a SaFe(08)
2007 – *No Country for Old Men*	Old Men carrying SaCKs(07)
2006 – *The Departed*	The Departed lying in SewaGe(06)
2005 – *Crash*	A Crashed SaiL(05)
2004 – *Million Dollar Baby*	Million Dollar Baby is SoRe(04)
2003 – *The Lord of the Rings: The Return of the King*	Gollum fighting SaM(03) in Return of the King
2002 – *Chicago*	Chicago and SiN(02)

(continued)

Oscar winners	Reference story (examples)
2001 – *A Beautiful Mind*	A Beautiful Mind that is **SaD**(01)
2000 – *Gladiator*	Gladiator covered in **SauCe**(00)
1999 – *American Beauty*	American Beauty is a **BaBe**(99)
1998 – *Shakespeare in Love*	Shakespeare at a **BuFfet**(98)
1997 – *Titanic*	Titanic is **BiG**(97) or **ePiC**(97)
1996 – *The English Patient*	The English Patient is **PoSH**(96)
1995 – *Braveheart*	Braveheart does **BaLLet**(95)
1994 – *Forrest Gump*	Forrest Gump loves a **PeaR**(94)
1993 – *Schindler's List*	Schindler's List goes **BooM**(93)
1992 – *Unforgiven*	Unforgiven ends up in the **BiN**(92)
1991 – *The Silence of the Lambs*	Hannibal is scary with his **BaT**(91)
1990 – *Dances with Wolves*	Dancing Wolves playing the **BaSS**(90)
1989 – *Driving Miss Daisy*	Driving Miss Daisy is **PHoeBe**(89)
1988 – *Rain Man*	Rain Man in **ViVa**(88) Las Vegas
1987 – *The Last Emperor*	The Last Emperor in the **FoG**(87)

Oscar winners	Reference story (examples)
1986 – *Platoon*	Platoon on a VoyaGe(86)
1985 – *Out of Africa*	FaLL(85) Out of Africa
1984 – *Amadeus*	Amadeus playing on a FeRRy(84)
1983 – *Terms of Endearment*	Shirley MacLaine of huge FaMe(83)
1982 – *Gandhi*	Gandhi surrounded by FaNs(82)
1981 – *Chariots of Fire*	Chariots of Fire racing bareFooT(81)
1980 – *Ordinary People*	Ordinary Person with an extraordinary FaCe(80)
1979 – *Kramer vs. Kramer*	Kramers fighting in a CaB(79)
1978 – *The Deer Hunter*	The Deer Hunter gun scene set in a café(78)
1977 – *Annie Hall*	Annie Hall baking a CaKe(77)
1976 – *Rocky*	Rocky in a CaGe(76)
1975 – *One Flew over the Cuckoo's Nest*	Nicholson with a CLaw(75)
1974 – *The Godfather, Part II*	The Godfather in a ChoiR(74)
1973 – *The Sting*	The Sting covered in GuM(73)
1972 – *The Godfather*	The Godfather in aGoNy(72)
1971 – *The French Connection*	The French CaDDy(71)

(*continued*)

Oscar winners	Reference story (your stories)
1970 – Patton	
1969 – Midnight Cowboy	
1968 – Oliver!	
1967 – In the Heat of the Night	
1966 – A Man for All Seasons	
1965 – The Sound of Music	
1964 – My Fair Lady	
1963 – Tom Jones	
1962 – Lawrence of Arabia	
1961 – West Side Story	
1960 – The Apartment	
1959 – Ben-Hur	
1958 – Gigi	
1957 – The Bridge on the River Kwai	
1956 – Around the World in 80 Days	
1955 – Marty	
1954 – On the Waterfront	
1953 – From Here to Eternity	
1952 – The Greatest Show on Earth	
1951 – An American in Paris	
1950 – All About Eve	
1949 – All the King's Men	
1948 – Hamlet	
1947 – Gentleman's Agreement	
1946 – The Best Years of Our Lives	

Oscar winners	Reference story (your stories)
1945 – *The Lost Weekend*	
1944 – *Going My Way*	
1943 – *Casablanca*	
1942 – *Mrs. Miniver*	
1941 – *How Green Was My Valley*	
1940 – *Rebecca*	
1939 – *Gone with the Wind*	
1938 – *You Can't Take It with You*	
1937 – *The Life of Emile Zola*	
1936 – *The Great Ziegfeld*	
1935 – *Mutiny on the Bounty*	
1934 – *It Happened One Night*	
1932/33 – *Cavalcade*	
1931/32 – *Grand Hotel*	
1930/31 – *Cimarron*	
1929/30 – *All Quiet on the Western Front*	
1928/29 – *The Broadway Melody*	
1927/28 – *Wings*	

History

History is all about stories and is therefore a great fit for creative memorization. To help with the process there is usually a wealth of imagery online that can be used in your reference stories. The statue of Pytheas for example could be used as the image for Pytheas; if you need an image to help remember his name, you might simply imagine him eating a pie – with repetition you will just know the state is Pytheas.

Action – Historical facts

Time limit: 30 minutes

With historical facts it can be useful to create your reference stories to begin with and then choose one key image to store on a memory network. This will allow you to run through in sequence. When you see Pytheas on the memory node, your memory recalls the reference story of Pytheas sailing around the British Isles.

This also has the benefit of being able to memorize information as and when you need it and arrange it in a structured sequence at a later date.

Example

Memory node 1: Pytheas → remember reference story

Memory node 2: Camulodunum

Memory node 3: Hadrian

British timeline	Reference story (examples)
330–320BC – Pytheas of Massilia (now Marseilles) – Greek merchant and explorer circumnavigated the British Isles – produced the first written record of the islands.	**Pytheas** (statue) sailing around the **British Isles** with a gigantic **written record** of the islands. On the ship is **MuMS**(330) **MiNCe**(320).
AD43 – British capital Camulodunum (Colchester) falls to the Romans and Emperor Claudius.	Camulodunum is being held in the enormous clawed hand of Claudius from **RoMe**(43).
AD122 – Emperor Hadrian orders the construction of a wall across northern Britain.	Hadrian's Wall is covered in **TaNNiN**(122).
843 – Kenneth MacAlpine unites Scots and Picts in a 'kingdom of Scotland'.	Kenneth MacAlpine on a **FaRM**(843) hugging a Scot and a Pict forming a Kingdom.

(continued)

British timeline	Reference story (your stories)
1042 – Edward the Confessor becomes King of England.	
1190 – Richard I joins the Third Crusade.	
23 August 1305 – Scottish rebel William Wallace is executed by the English.	
1315–1322 – Millions die in the Great European Famine.	
1337 – Hundred Years War between England and France begins.	
1509 – Henry VII dies and is succeeded by Henry VIII.	
1580 – Francis Drake arrives at Plymouth after circumnavigating the world.	
1651 – Oliver Cromwell defeats Charles II at the Battle of Worcester.	
1694 – Bank of England is established.	
1768 – Captain James Cook leads his first expedition to the Pacific.	
1807 – Britain abolishes the slave trade.	
1903 – Women's Social and Political Union is formed to campaign for women's suffrage.	

Source: http://www.bbc.co.uk/history

Literature

As a way to begin priming yourself for the works of Shakespeare, first start by memorizing the titles and most likely dates of his plays (it is not really known with any certainty when each play was written but the list below is based on widely held opinion). You could choose to create a memory network on which to store them. You then have the option to associate the relevant characters and plot to each play.

Action – Shakespeare

Time limit: 1 hour

▶ Create a memory network that you can chunk into three (comedies, tragedies and histories).

▶ All comedies in this list except the last four are dated 15__; you therefore need to associate only the last two digits to the name of the play (you can use this same idea with the other sections).

Comedies	Reference story (examples)
1591 – *The Comedy of Errors*	BaT(91) a **Comedy** with lots of **Errors**
1591 – *The Two Gentlemen of Verona*	BaTs(91) being handed to **Two** handy looking **Gentlemen**
1594 – *The Merchant of Venice*	Lots of BeeR(94) being drunk by the **Merchant** in **Venice**
1594 – *A Midsummer Night's Dream*	An **Ass** drinking BeeR(94)
1594 – *The Taming of the Shrew*	**Taming** the **Shrew** with BeeR(94)
1598 – *All's Well That Ends Well*	A slice of BeeF(98) that has ended **well**
1598 – *As You Like It*	**You** like this BeeF(98)
1598 – *Love's Labour's Lost*	BeeF(98) looking for its **lost love**
1599 – *The Merry Wives of Windsor*	The **Merry Wives of Windsor**, with lots of BaBies(99)

Comedies	Reference story (examples)
1599 – *Twelfth Night, or What You Will*	A BaBe(99) all alone on **Twelfth Night**
1600 – *Much Ado About Nothing*	**Much Ado** about SauCe(00) being spilt
1604 – *Measure for Measure*	**MeasuringSiR(04)**
1610 – *The Winter's Tale*	In **Winter** a **Tale** made of DaiSies(10)
1611 – *The Tempest*	**Temp**ted by **TeD(11)**

Tragedies	Reference story (your stories)
1591 – *The Tragedy of Romeo and Juliet*	
1592 – *The Tragedy of Titus Andronicus*	
1599 – *The Tragedy of Hamlet, Prince of Denmark*	
1599 – *The Tragedy of Julius Caesar*	
1602 – *The History of Troilus and Cressida*	
1604 – *The Tragedy of Othello, The Moor of Venice*	
1605 – *The Tragedy of King Lear*	
1606 – *The Tragedy of Macbeth*	
1607 – *The Life of Timon of Athens*	
1607 – *The Tragedy of Antony and Cleopatra*	
1608 – *Pericles, Prince of Tyre*	

(continued)

Tragedies	Reference story (your stories)

1608 – *The Tragedy of Coriolanus*

1610 – *The Tragedy of Cymbeline*

1613 – *The Two Noble Kinsmen*

Histories	Reference story (your stories)

1592 – *The First Part of King Henry the Sixth*

1593 – *The Tragedy of Richard the Third, With the Landing of Earl Richmond and the Battle at Bosworth Field*

1593 – *The Second Part of King Henry the Sixth*

1595 – *The Third Part of King Henry the Sixth*

1596 – *The Life and Death of King John*

1597 – *The Tragedy of King Richard the Second*

1597 – *The First Part of King Henry the Fourth*

1597 – *The Second Part of King Henry the Fourth*

1599 – *The Life of Henry the Fifth*

1613 – *The Life of King Henry the Eighth*

Science and nature

THE BRAIN

The brain is a complex structure of neuronal networks, entwining, overlapping and connecting to form specific brain structures. Although not essential in order for you to improve your memory, being able to remember what some of those structures are, and their purpose, will prime you to build future knowledge about the brain.

Action – Journey through the brain

Time limit: 15 minutes
These represent a few structures of the brain and some of their functions. Create a memory network consisting of three locations and the appropriate number of items in each location.

Brain structures	Reference story (examples)
Location 1: The brain stem (connects the brain and spinal cord)	Stem connecting the brain and spinal cord
Item 1: Medulla – respiration, heart, gastrointestinal functions	Medal, breathing with a beating heart
Item 2: Pons – interconnects brain stem and cerebellum	Pins, connecting the stem and small brain
Item 3: Midbrain – control of movement	Midfielder controlling movement

Brain structures	Reference story (your stories)
Location 2: Cerebellum – sensory motor co-ordination, seems to play an important role in learning	

(continued)

Location 3: Cerebrum – (forebrain) overlies the lower structures

Item 1: Thalamus – relay station for sensory experience that projects to cerebral cortex

Item 2: Hypothalamus – master control centre for emotion

Item 3: Amygdala (limbic) – emotional learning, fear, importance; involved Pavlovian conditioning, influences how memory is stored

Item 4: Hippocampus (limbic) – key role in forming declarative memories

Item 5: Fornix (limbic) – interconnecting structures of the limbic system

Item 6: Basal ganglia – integration of motor activity

Item 7: Cerebral cortex – covers the cerebrum; high-level brain functions – thoughts, reasoning, planning, decision-making and imagination

PERIODIC TABLE

Earlier in this book you had a taster of how to remember the elements of the periodic table using the chain method. It can also be helpful to use a memory network onto which you can associate more information in the future.

Action – The elements

Time limit: 30 minutes

▶ Create a memory network for as many elements as you wish to remember (at least 30).
▶ Use the number of the node of the memory network to represent the atomic number. This means you will not have to create a separate image for the number, e.g. Boron will be on your fifth node, therefore its atomic number is 5.
▶ Create one image per element.

Elements of the periodic table

Atomic no. – Symbol – Element	Reference story (examples)
1 – H – Hydrogen	Hydrogen bomb
2 – He – Helium	Helium balloon
3 – Li – Lithium	Lithium floating in water
4 – Be – Beryllium	Bee
5 – B – Boron	Boar
6 – C – Carbon	Car
7 – N – Nitrogen	Nitro
8 – O – Oxygen	Oxygen mask
9 – F – Fluorine	Flower reacting violently
10 – Ne – Neon	Neon sign
11 – Na – Sodium	Soda
12 – Mg – Magnesium	Magazine
13 – Al – Aluminium	Aluminium
14 – Si – Silicon	Silly cone
15 – P – Phosphorus	Fozzy

(continued)

Atomic no. – Symbol – Element	Reference story (examples)
16 – S – Sulphur	Smelly Sulphur
17 – Cl – Chlorine	Chlorine gas
18 – Ar – Argon	Aga oven
19 – K – Potassium	Pot
20 – Ca – Calcium	Milk
21 – Sc – Scandium	Scan
22 – Ti – Titanium	Titanium clubs
23 – V – Vanadium	Van
24 – Cr – Chromium	Chrome wheels
25 – Mn – Manganese	Man on knees
26 – Fe – Iron	Iron man
27 – Co – Cobalt	Cobbles
28 – Ni – Nickel	A nickel
29 – Cu – Copper	Copper
30 – Zn – Zinc	Piece of zinc

Sports and leisure

Depending on the circles you frequent, the ability to pull out facts about sport can be a useful one. As well as demonstrating your knowledge, it is probably one of the more fun areas to be able to share information about.

If you are reading this before the Olympic Games 2012, notice how it changes your focus when you know the exact record athletes are trying to beat. If you are reading it after, you will be able to use this as a benchmark.

Action – World records at the Olympics

Time limit: 30 minutes

If you choose to put these on a memory network, it may make sense to create one specifically for world records achieved at the Beijing Olympic Games in 2008.

World records at the 2008 Olympics	Reference stories (examples)
100 metres (athletics) 9.69 seconds Usain Bolt (Jamaica)	**Usain Bolt** wearing **Jamaican** flag doing the 100 metres like Charlie **CHaPlin**(69)
200 metres individual medley (swimming) 1:54.23 Michael Phelps (USA)	**Michael Phelps** wearing **USA** flag swimming against Swans with Medals (number shape system **2** – 200 metres), who were paid a **DoLLaR**(1:54) from **NeMo**(23) to take a dive
Men's 4 km team pursuit (cycling) 3:53.31 Ed Clancy, Bradley Wiggins, Paul Manning, Geraint Thomas (UK)	*Note: Use the 'real people' and memorize their names separately.* A **4**seater bike, with **Ed**, **Bradley**, **Paul** and **Geraint** hanging off different parts, they e**MaiL** (3:5) a **MohaMaD** (3:31)
Men's 85 kg total (weightlifting) 394 kg Andrei Rybakou (Belarus)	**Andrei** lifting huge dumb**Bells** (Belarus) on top of the Eiffel(85) Tower in front of the e**MPiRe**(394)
World records at the 2008 Olympics	Reference story (your stories)
Men's 4 × 100 metres relay (athletics) 37.10 Usain Bolt, Asafa Powell, Michael Frater, Nesta Carter (Jamaica)	

(continued)

World records at the 2008 Olympics	Reference story (your stories)
Women's 10 metre air rifle qualification (shooting) 400 Katerina Emmons (Czech Republic)	
Men's 100 metres breaststroke (swimming) 58.91 Kosuke Kitajima (Japan)	
Women's 69 kg total (weightlifting) 286 kg Liu Chunhong (China)	
Men's quadruple sculls (rowing) 5:36.20 Christopher Morgan, James McRae, Brendan Long, Daniel Noonan (Australia)	
Women's 3,000 metres steeplechase (athletics) 8:58.81 Gulnara Samitova-Galkina (Russia)	

RECIPES

The ability to remember recipes has a real practical value in everyday life. With creative memorization you can use memory networks to initially memorize the ingredients needed for a particular recipe and then use a combination of visual cues and physical rehearsal to remember the actual preparation. By going through this process, you are engaging several different types of memory: semantic, episodic and procedural.

Action – Spanish chicken and chorizo (by Phil Poole)

Time limit: 30 minutes
This will break down into two parts:

- ▶ Create a memory network and memorize the ingredients.
- ▶ Create a set of visual cues using the chain method that you can use to physically and mentally rehearse the preparation in order to consolidate this recipe to memory.

Ingredients	Reference story (examples)
4 chicken breasts	**Chicken Breasts on a Door (4)**
1 chorizo ring	**a Chorizo Ring**
1 can of chopped tomatoes	**Chopped Tomatoes**
3 bay leaves	**Bay Leaves** on a **Tree (3)**
1-2 tablespoon of paprika	Tablespoon of **Paprika**
1/4 teaspoon of chilli	Teaspoon of **Chilli**

For the basil and lime mayonnaise	Reference story (your stories)
70ml (1/4 cup) of dry sherry or vermouth (recommend. Tio pepe)	
1 red pepper	
1 yellow pepper	
1 red onion	
1-2 cloves garlic	
2 packets of Rocket leaves	
1 casserole dish or large saucepan	
1 tablespoon of olive oil	
Pinch of pepper and salt	

To serve	Reference story (your stories)
For something more substantial serve with crunchy fresh bread or garlic bread if you are feeling really decedent.	

Source: www.welovenicethings.com

Preparation method

For each instruction use the chain method to set your visual cues and rehearse preparing the meal.

▶ Slice the peppers and onion roughly, crush the garlic clove(s), slice the chicken breasts into two chunks.

▶ Put the casserole dish on the hob on medium heat and add the olive oil; once heated add the chicken breast and brown on all sides for 2-3 minutes. Remove to a spare plate.

▶ Add the garlic, peppers and onion to the oil and cook in the oil until soft (about 3-5 minutes).

▶ Add the chicken breast back in along with the chopped tomatoes and sherry. Also add the paprika, chilli powder, salt and pepper. Once the mixture is bubbling, reduce heat so it is simmering and place lid on.

▶ After 20 minutes stir the mixture and taste, add more paprika and (sparingly chilli) to taste, simmer for another 20 minutes with lid on.

▶ The tomato sauce will now have reduced to a lovely gloopy mess. Slice the chorizo ring and add to dish and simmer for another 5 minutes with lid on.

▶ Remove from heat, add a bed of rocket leaves on each serving dish, add 2-3 chicken pieces on top and then add a mixture of the tomato sauce, peppers, onion and chorizo on and around the leaves and serve.

On the same memory network after the ingredients connect these three chains:

1 *Imagine slicing the rough peppers and onion who crush garlic over the two chunks of chicken.*
2 *A huge casserole dish with oil has a chicken breast swimming in it that is brown, it jumps onto a plate.*
3 *Garlic, peppers and onion jump into the hot oil and start swimming with MaiL (3-5).*
4 *Chicken jumps out of the MaiL and puts chopped tomotoes into a bottle of sherry, the sherry is itchy and covered in paprika, chilli, salt and pepper. Everything starts bubbling, you throw a lid on it.*
5 *A NaSa (20) ship crashes into the lid and starts sipping the contents*
6 *It takes slices of chorizo and covers with a SaiL (05).*
7 *You pick it up and drop on a bed of rocket leaves, the chicken jumps on top, the sauce dripping around it.*

In practice

Put your knowledge to the test and see how well you score on the 'How to Remember' pub quiz.

Action – Pub quiz

Time limit: 10 minutes
Test your knowledge with our pub quiz.

1   Which ocean has the deepest trench?
2   How many bay leaves are in Spanish chicken and chorizo?
3   Out of the first 30 elements on the periodic table, name how many have a symbol starting with the letter C.
4   Name the four athletes who broke the world record for the men's 4 × 100 metres relay at the Beijing Olympics.
5   Is it the hypothalamus or the hippocampus that has a key role in forming declarative memories?
6   Which three plays is Shakespeare thought to have written in 1591?
7   What year were the hills alive with the *Sound of Music* at the Oscars?
8   Where and in what year did Francis Drake arrive after circumnavigating the world?
9   Put these mountains in order of highest to lowest: Nanga Parbat, Kanchenjunga, Annapurna.
10 What element comes after iron in the periodic table and what is its symbol and number?
11 Which of the following parts of the brain controls sensory motor skills: amygdala, cerebellum, medulla?
12 How much mayonnaise is needed to make basil and lime mayonnaise?
13 Was the women's 3,000 metres steeplechase world record set by Gulnara Samitova-Galkina, Liu Chunhong or Katerina Emmons?
14 When is Shakespeare thought to have written *Hamlet* and what year did the film win the Oscar?
15 In which year did the English execute William Wallace and in what year did the film about his life win the Oscar?
16 How many histories did Shakespeare write about a Henry?
17 Britain abolished the slave trade in which year: 1807, 1808, or 1809?
18 How many minutes do you simmer the Spanish chicken and chorizo for?
19 Usain Bolt set a world record at the Beijing Olympics, running the 100 metres in how many seconds?
20 *The Godfather* won the Oscar for best film in 1974, 1973, or 1972?

KEYS TO A GREAT MEMORY

▶ Learn and grow future general knowledge by sowing the seeds today.

▶ Take creative memorization to the next level by immersing yourself in the memorization of complex facts, numbers and dates.

▶ There are various methods for remembering general knowledge across a variety of areas: geography, entertainment, history, literature, science and nature, and sports and leisure.

▶ You can use creative memorization to remember the ingredients and also how to cook your favourite recipes.

12

Programming to remember: Take control of your memory

In this chapter you will learn:
- *how to remember where you've put things using mental tags*
- *games to condition your memory*
- *how to programme future memories.*

There will always be things that we forget, whether it is where we've put something or the 'important' task we were 'supposed' to do. A lot of the time this is due to lack of attention or our attention being diverted. However, there are things we can do to increase our awareness and remember those things that make us go 'doh!'

The past: Where did I put my keys?

It's a cliché, but the thought behind it stands true. I am sure that at one or perhaps many times in your life you have experienced the 'Where did I put my keys?' scenario. It can be fairly frustrating; you 'know' you left your keys on the kitchen table, you search everywhere for them, someone must have moved them, you search everywhere again, you think about what you were wearing last time you had them, ten minutes go by and now you are late, then your partner finds them on the bookshelf, 'Ah, now I remember.'

There is a strategy you can play with that will make a shift in how you think about this specific scenario, how you deal with it and the outcome. The strategy is simple and you have more than enough skills to put it into practice.

In effect you are aiming to set yourself up to remember. To do this there has to be a conscious effort when you put something down (your keys in this case); by conditioning yourself to do this, over time it will become an unconscious habit.

The outcome of this is that more and more you will be able to remember where you put things. You may find that when this starts to work for you, you use the same or a similar technique to remember other things that happen, not just where you put things but small moments or events. While moments and events can be memorable within themselves, by mentally 'tagging' them, you can make them stand out in your memory.

Action – Creating your tag

Time limit: 2 minutes
The idea of this 'Action' is that you start to condition yourself to remember things you've done in the past. Start small and just try this every time you put something down that you will need later.

▶ Create a tag-word – this could be something as simple as 'down'; practise saying it out loud in a specific way.
▶ Create a physical action to go with this tag-word – you might touch the object with two fingers in a specific way.
▶ Create an image you can see in your mind – you might imagine an alien substance reaching up from wherever the object is and grabbing it down tightly.
▶ To put this into practice fire off all three things at the same time.

Example

Try this with your phone or keys: put the item down on the table top, then as you touch it with your two fingers and say the word 'down' imagine the alien substance grabbing it – this should all happen fairly instantaneously. Do this five times.

Another option is to make something up on the spot. You put your keys down beside the microwave – imagine they go smashing through the microwave (the microwave screams); this image will stand out in your mind when you next think of your keys.

When you next think of your phone or keys, you will remember this moment and therefore remember where they are. The problem is that you may forget to do this, which is why you need to condition yourself to do it without thinking. You can do this by taking one to three items that you know you put down at least three or four times a day, and spend the next seven days tagging those items; for this to work you have to make a conscious effort.

Action – Find the blank

Time limit: 10 mins, played over the course of 1 week

There is a simple game you can play that will help condition your memory in this area. It's also fun – and if you are the person who gets asked a lot 'Where's my _____?', you will love this game. It is aimed at couples or families; you could play it on your own but you would always win.

Rules

- The game lasts a week, starting on Monday and finishing on Sunday.
- The names of the players are written on a piece of A4 paper and pinned to a wall.
- Whenever anyone says 'Where's my _____?' or words to that effect, they have 5 minutes in which to find it. If they find it, then nothing is marked on the board; but if they don't, an X goes down (maximum of three Xs in one day or there is a consequence – you decide).
- If they haven't found it after 5 minutes, everyone else joins in the search; you get an extra life if you find it (a star or a tick) that you can use to get rid of a future X you may pick up.
- The person with the most Xs at the end of the week gets a penalty – they might pay for a meal out or a movie, or if you have children you could dream up some fun chores

If you have a family, this can be quite amusing; the interesting thing is how quickly you get conditioned to remember where you have put stuff. Combine this with the tag-word strategy and you will find that forgetting where things are is a thing of the past.

Play the timeline

If you find that even with tagging you are still not able to remember, next time you forget where something is, rather than looking all over the house, take a moment, breathe deeply, let yourself relax and then ask the question 'Where are my _____?' Ask the question with the expectation that you will get an answer and then let your mind drift and take you back to the point where you last remember having them; remember this time in detail. When you have that picture clear in your mind, start to play the timeline forward as far as you can until you remember where they last were.

With this technique you may find that half-way through, the location of your item suddenly pops into your mind. You are essentially looking for connections, trying to spark off the same neuronal pathways that were created when you put that item down.

The future: Don't forget the milk!

There are many occasions when you want to remember something at a specific time in the future; in order to do this something has to trigger that memory. By creating future memory through creative memorization, you can effectively make suggestions to your unconscious mind, programming yourself to remember the thing you want to do at an event in the future.

You could think of it like getting notifications pushed to your phone; in the same way, your unconscious can metaphorically 'push' actions to your conscious when triggered by an event.

Action – Creating your anchor

Time limit: 5 minutes
This technique works in a similar way to the technique for creating a tag. The difference being that rather than create a memory for where something is right now, we will remember it at a future time. With your anchor you are creating a memory for a future event that will be unconsciously triggered when that event happens.

Example

You want to remember to pick up a pint of milk when you finish work.

▶ Create an anchor word – let's use 'Remember'. Practise saying it aloud in a specific way.

▶ Create a physical action to go with it – maybe a 'click' of the fingers.

▶ Create a future memory – imagine as you step off your train and put your ticket through the ticket barrier you see an enormous pint of milk running up to hug you.

▶ Once the image is clear in your mind, fire off all three together – see the story and as soon as the enormous milk comes into it say 'Remember milk' and click your fingers on the word 'milk'.

You may find that, as you get off the train, milk will pop into your head before you get to the ticket barrier. If this happens, it's important that you keep it in your mind until you get there. More often than not the memory will be triggered either before or just at the right moment.

Like the first technique, this one will take some practice: you should aim to use it at least one to five times a day for the first seven days in order to condition it into your way of thinking.

Insight

Although this technique is really simple, I still find it impressive when just at the right moment the memory pops into my head. One of the side-effects of both of these techniques is that they create some very strong references in your ability to remember. With strong references you create strong beliefs and with a belief in your abilities your memory will continue to improve.

KEYS TO A GREAT MEMORY

▶ Practise using the tag technique: fire off a physical action, key word and visual image simultaneously to remember where you have put things.

▶ Take the seven-day challenge and condition yourself to tag where you put your relevant possessions without thinking.

▶ Play the 'Find the Blank' game as a fun way to improve your skills with the tag technique.

▶ Try using the timeline technique, taking yourself back to a time when you last had the object you have forgotten and imagine running the timeline forward.

▶ Create an anchor for remembering things you have to do in the future by having a key word, physical action and a future memory. Program yourself by firing off all three together.

▶ Practise programming yourself with future memories.

13

Information overload: Strategies for remembering

In this chapter you will learn:
- *techniques for filtering and remembering relevant information*
- *how to remember articles and latest news*
- *a process for remembering entire books*
- *how to rapidly capture details from meetings, presentations and conferences.*

Dealing with information overload is more than just increasing your capacity to remember. In a day-to-day sense it is more about filtering what is relevant, planning your time and prioritizing according to the value you or others will get. You will have information you want to consume, learn and use in different areas of your life. That could be your own personal development or that of your family; new skills or games; day-to-day emails from work; keeping up to date with the latest news; remembering facts from lectures, meetings or seminars; reading books and magazines on your favourite subject; or searching the endless amount of material available on the internet.

Emails and social media

Emails and social media can be a major contributor to information that comes our way. In the age of social media, information is also transferred across different mediums such as Twitter, Facebook and the ever growing Google+. With over 29 million users in the UK on Facebook at the time of writing and the way we consume information changing with mobile devices and tablets becoming the norm, the ability to access information anywhere adds to the opportunities available to us at any time. Creative memorization can play a role in supporting you with these media and adding value to what you can take away and use.

SETTING YOURSELF UP

It is a simple technique, but because of the nature of email and social media, with their addictive qualities, lots of people will find the urge to continually check if anything new has arrived, whether someone has replied to a previous email or post, whether there is anything important to respond to. At times this isn't a problem; however, during the course of a working day, depending on your career, you may find you receive a lot of emails, some that require direct action, some that require something to be remembered and others that are merely there for information purposes.

In order to set yourself up with an easier task, try chunking your day into times when you will respond to emails and times when you won't: morning, before lunch and late afternoon can work well. There might be a concern here that you will miss something 'important' but if it is important enough, it is more than likely to come to your attention. Avoid any other activity during these times, reprioritize, push back and stick to this rule. Let people know what you are doing so you can set their expectations and also give them an opportunity to contact you via other means if it has a higher priority. Depending on your career, setting yourself up in this way may not really be an issue, but if you find that emails or updates of any kind are getting in your way think about a similar model you can put in place that would help.

FILTERING AND REMEMBERING

Once you have pre-allocated set times to work through email, build in time to memorize any relevant information and key actions: these can usually be placed on a temporary memory network. It is useful to memorize only actions that are of importance for that day or information you would like to refer back to at a later date.

Here is a guide to how you could utilize mind maps, speed reading and creative memorization to filter out and remember relevant information:

▶ Set up your filters for what is important and/or urgent for you today, this week, this month (this should be at a high level, not every task). This will help prime you for what is relevant.
▶ Update an Actions mind map with a branch that has your filters (software such as iMindMap or handwritten whiteboard mind maps are ideal).

- You can choose to add your filters to an Actions memory network.
- Speed read your emails and any relevant documents attached, respond where necessary and flag any that require you to remember information or take any other action.
- Add anything you need to remember or do to your Actions mind map (before).
- Decide what filter branch they need to go on – Day, Week, Month (after).
- Memorize and action what you need to do today.

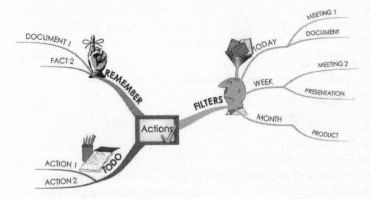

Figure 13.1 Actions mind map – before (created using ThinkBuzan'siMindMap http://www.thinkbuzan.com).

Figure 13.2 Actions mind map – after (created using ThinkBuzan'siMindMap http:// www.thinkbuzan.com).

Documents and articles

Keeping up to date with knowledge and current research is what can give you 'the edge', getting you known as an expert in your field and a go-to person in your area.

Action – The article challenge

Time limit: 30 minutes

▶ Look for the key points in this article and use creative memorization to remember those facts: you can choose to use a memory network or the chain method or a combination.

Laughter leads to insight

Happy moods facilitate aha! moments

Stumped by a crossword puzzle? Try taking a break to watch a funny TV show. Recent research shows that people in a lighthearted mood more often have eureka moments of sudden inspiration.

Karuna Subramaniam, then at Northwestern University, and her colleagues found that boosting the mood of volunteers increased their likelihood of having an aha! moment that helped solve a word association puzzle. Those who watched a Robin Williams comedy special did measurably better at the task using insight than those who watched a quantum electronics talk or a scary movie. The games, in which players must find a word that connects three seemingly unrelated words, have been used for decades to demonstrate creative problem solving.

In the brain, sudden insight is accompanied by increased activity in the brain's anterior cingulated cortex (ACC) prior to solving each problem. The region is involved in regulating attention; in problem solving, it seems to work in conjunction with other brain areas either to stay focused on a particular strategy or to switch to a new one. Subramaniam found with functional MRI that people in a positive mood had more ACC activity going in to the task, which probably helped prepare the brain to find novel solutions. Participants who watched anxiety-producing movies such as

The Shining, *however, showed less activity in the ACC and less creativity in solving the puzzles.*

Elizabeth King Humphrey

Scientific American Mind magazine, May 2011

- ▶ Create a mind map capturing your main thoughts (this was a rapid two-minute capturing stage).
- ▶ Colour in and decorate the map as you recite out loud in your own words.
  - ▶ Extract key images
  - ▶ Happy mood
  - ▶ Karuna Subramaniam
  - ▶ Robin Williams
  - ▶ Word task
  - ▶ ACC Aha! solutions
- ▶ Create a chain – imagine this on the backdrop of a classroom in *Dead Poets' Society* with a group on each side of the room. **Karuna** and **Robin Williams** are in a **happy mood** as they take **three words** attached to a chain and **link** them to a bottle of **solution** with a **signet – Aha!** says Williams.
- ▶ Recite the article in your own words without referring to the mind map.

Figure 13.3 Mind map sketch.

News

Since news stories are more about what is happening now than what happened last month, last year or even last week, if you want to have the latest news logged in your memory bank, it is a quick and easy process.

Action – News headlines

Time limit: 15 minutes
- ▶ Create a memory network for the latest news stories and chunk into your favourite categories:
  - ▶ World
  - ▶ UK
  - ▶ Politics
  - ▶ Sport
  - ▶ Entertainment
- ▶ You will probably only need ten nodes per chunk.

Whether you get your news from the TV, phone, computer or newspaper, while reading, listening or watching the news, do the following:

- ▶ Create a reference story for the relevant news article.

In the news today, 7 August 2011, there is a story of an aged Andy Warhol sculpture, depicting what he might have looked like had he still been alive. It was unveiled to mark his 83rd birthday.

- ▶ Speed read the article (if reading).
- ▶ Imagine the **statue** of **Andy Warhol** who once said, 'In the future everyone will be FaMous(83) for 15 minutes'.
- ▶ Dial up the intensity of this reference story so it becomes logged in your memory.
- ▶ Now decide whether you want to associate it with the latest news in your entertainment network; if so, connect Andy Warhol's statue to your first node.
- ▶ Once you fill up the nodes you have created in each category, simply erase the information on them and start again; you will find that with some news stories you will add more detail as they grow over time, for others they might only last a day as they become less relevant.

Books

Memorizing a book requires a combination of techniques; how much work you have to do depends on the level of detail you want from it. You have the option to use all or a subset of the strategies that are available to you in order to meet your purpose and put what you learn to use.

Having gone through the reading strategies chapter, you will know that the steps include:

- ▶ Create purpose and direction
- ▶ Prime yourself through previewing
- ▶ Capture the 10,000-foot view with a mind map
- ▶ Speed read for comprehension and learning.

EIGHT-STEP STRATEGY FOR REMEMBERING ENTIRE BOOKS

With creative memorization there are four more steps (in bold type below) we can add to increase speed and retention. All of the following is done through the lens of the learning cycle – taking in sensory input, reflecting, abstracting and actioning.

Steps

1 Create purpose and direction
2 Prime yourself through preview
3 Capture the 10,000-foot view with a mind map
4 **Construct your mental scaffolding, memorize relevant table of contents (TOC) and glossary terms**
5 Speed read for comprehension and learning
6 **Create detailed mind map of book**
7 **Memorize facts and details**
8 **Action it!**

- ▶ Once you know 'why' you are reading the book, you will have a clear purpose and direction. (2 minutes)
- ▶ Having a clear purpose will make it easier when you preview, priming your attention for relevant information that catches your eye. (5 minutes)
- ▶ Create your 10,000-foot view mind map; use this time to rapidly put your mind map in place and reflect on what you already know while you capture some initial questions. (10 minutes)

Figure 13.4 Steps mind map (created using ThinkBuzan'siMindMap
http://www.thinkbuzan.com).

- ▶ Construct your mental scaffolding, decide how much of the
  book's table of contents (TOC) and terms in the glossary to
  memorize, depending on how familiar the material is. This may
  not always be necessary: a good rule of thumb is if it's a new
  topic, memorize at least some of the unfamiliar terms. Going
  through this process will set you up to speed read and allow you
  to mentally run through the book after you have read it, making
  more internal connections. (10 minutes–1 hour, depending on
  complexity). *Limit yourself to an hour maximum for this phase.*
- ▶ Speed reading is where you will gain a deeper understanding of
  the material, reflecting on what you know internally and how
  it relates to other information you have had externally. It is
  important that you work on the strategies discussed in the speed
  reading section in order to avoid back-skipping, regression and
  Subvocalization. (15 minutes–2 hours) *If it is over 2 hours take a
  break before continuing.*
- ▶ When your reading is complete, the initial memorization you
  did of the index can help in creating a detailed mind map. Aim
  to do this from memory and only refer back to the book when
  necessary. It doesn't matter if you make mistakes, you can cross-
  reference your mind map when you construct your memory
  network in the next phase. (15 minutes–2 hours)

▶ When your detailed mind map is in place, you can construct your memory network to remember any key facts and details. At this point you may need to refer back to the book (15 minutes–?). *The amount of time this takes will be dependent on your information.*

▶ The final essential step is to put what you have learned into action. This may take the form of a presentation or essay and, if it is a book that develops a skill, you put those skills into practice. Any action you take should be in keeping with your initial purpose. (Some books may not require all steps, it could be sufficient to set your purpose, preview, mind map and memorize some key facts – this could take as little as 30 minutes.

The amount of time you allocate will depend on your purpose and the level of detail you require. If you are doing a Masters degree, for example, there will be a much higher commitment of time; if you want to learn the latest project management skills from a new publication, your investment of time will be minimal.

Insight

In the beginning this can 'seem' like a lot to do. In actual fact the time taken is minimal compared with simply reading a book and you will receive the major benefit of being able to retain information over a long period of time. My advice would be to run through this process with three books that interest you, play with it and adapt the model to your own style.

With some books you will need to take more 'action' in order to gain enough comprehension. A good example of this might be programming. By reading a book and memorizing syntax and concepts, you could get to a point where you understand what is going on; however, you wouldn't be able to pick up a laptop and start creating functions and classes. It is not enough to understand the concepts; in order to be a proficient or even basic programmer, you need to be 'writing code'.

You will be the best person to know the level of understanding you need in order to do your job. If you are studying anatomy for the purpose of qualifying as a pilates instructor, your depth of knowledge would not need to be at the same level as someone who is qualifying as a physiotherapist.

Action – Memorize a book

Time limit: 2 hours

It is time to put what you know into practice and pull together all of the strategies you have explored to date to memorize information from a book that is relevant to you and will help you achieve some purpose.

- ▶ For this exercise you should limit yourself to two hours and go as far as you can within that time. If this is your first attempt, be aware that it will take time for you to make this second nature.
- ▶ Use the eight-step process outlined to memorize a book of your choice; follow the steps closely and at the end think about how you can adapt them and improve them to fit your own style.

Example of how to set up and use your memory networks

Here is an example of how you may use the creative memorization part of the memorizing a book process. We will use a chapter from Essential NLP: Teach Yourself, *by Steve Bavister and Amanda Vickers (content used in this example is sourced from the 2010 edition of this publication). This book is a good example to use as it is a combination of understanding concepts, remembering what they mean and how to use them, and then rehearsing putting them into practice in a real-world situation.*

Let us imagine that we have set up a memory network to memorize the table of contents: we will pull out a chapter to look at on Framing. At this point we have no idea what framing means.

We will be using a memory network that is a mixture of locations and items within those locations as our nodes. Chapter 14 will be in the 14th location, let us say this is your living room. Within the living room we will create six nodes (these are the items in your living room: the first item might be the sofa, the second the TV, the third the fireplace and so on), one node for each section in that chapter.

Next memorize the sections in the chapter.

Chapter 14: Frames, framing, reframing and parts	A FRAME in the middle of your living room
1 Understanding frames	Trying to understand
2 Reframing	Turn the frame around
3 Sleight of Mouth patterns	A big slight Mouth
4 Working with parts	Hammering Parts
5 Six-step reframing	Sticks (6) doing the time step
6 Negotiating between parts	Negotiating

Glossary	Reference Stories
Frame	A Big Frame covering Glastonbury
Reframing	Looking at the picture that from one direction looks like a witch and the other a beautiful woman

You glance through the glossary to prime yourself with one or two useful terms.

▶ A frame is the boundaries or constraints of an event or experience (I don't need to put this on a memory network as I am just memorizing a definition; I will only need it when I think of it).

▶ Reframing is transforming the meaning of something by changing the context or frame of reference.

The above steps will set you up for a good speed reading session.

After finishing, you create a mind map that is personal to you with your thoughts and questions.

Next you extract any relevant facts and details that make sense to store on a memory network: an example might be six-step reframing.

Bavister and Vickers talk about its use and how 'the "reframing" element involves separating the problematic behaviour from its

(continued)

positive intention, so that actions which on the surface appear to be negative are understood to have been trying to achieve something for the person'.

You would need to physically rehearse the six steps and then either create a chain of visual cues to remind you of the sequence of the steps or place the sequence of steps on a memory network.

You can continue this process of placing facts and details onto your memory networks or chains until you feel confident you have the required level of knowledge to fulfil your purpose.

When your memorization is complete you can move on to the final step: putting it into action.

Remembering books takes some effort and commitment; however, if you follow through, you can achieve some amazing results and each time you memorize a book you will find new ways of honing your skills.

Over the next four weeks, aim to practise these strategies on just one book a week. Start with a 'light' level of detail and, as you become more comfortable, build up the amount of facts and detail you consume.

Conferences

It is likely that at some point you will attend a lecture, a presentation, a seminar or a conference. When it comes to capturing, consuming, comprehending and remembering, the strategies you have learned throughout this book are invaluable.

Previously, while exploring mind mapping, you saw how these strategies could be used to capture relevant information, using where possible pre-structured templates to get you kick-started. It must be understood, however, that in certain situations, such as seminars and conferences, sometimes there isn't time to use colour and add lots of symbols, codes and images there and then.

If you attend a conference, the chances are that you will be going to many different talks during the time it is running, with huge amounts of information coming your way. It pays to have a strategy not only to capture and understand but also to memorize key facts and details.

Action – Techniques for lectures and seminars

Time limit: 10 minutes
Look at the following scenario and outline which of the techniques you have practised to this point would be beneficial while watching and listening to a lecture or seminar.

▶ One-day conference – you are attending a conference in which there are 11 talks you wish to hear; each talk lasts between 20 minutes and one hour. Some of the topics don't particularly interest you but since you are being sent there by your employer it is important that you pick up information.

Example

▶ *Define your purpose for the day, what you hope to take from it and what you will be able to offer others, e.g. your team, work colleagues, etc.*

▶ *Prior to going, memorize a list of talks that you are hoping to hear that will help you with your purpose.*

▶ *On the day, mind map all of your sessions. If you enjoy blogging, you can use the map as a reference for your blog and also upload the map for others.*

▶ *Consolidate the day onto one mind map; look for connections across all of your maps.*

▶ *Create a memory network for the event and memorize any 'key take aways' and speakers.*

Insight
One of my experiences of how powerful mind maps are was at a conference called the Future of Web Apps. A speaker came on at the last minute as someone had dropped out; she had no slides and started giving a presentation on Operant Conditioning, comparing this with several websites. While mapping I was also reflecting on my own experiences and abstracting how I would apply this in the future.

Figure 13.5 Rapid mind map from the Future of Web Apps Conference, 2008.

KEYS TO A GREAT MEMORY

▶ Use mind maps and creative memorization to help filter and remember important tasks. Pre-allocate time to deal with email and social media.

▶ Practise rapid mind mapping and the chain method to quickly consume and remember documents and articles.

▶ Keep up to date with the latest news stories utilizing categorized memory networks, speed reading articles and creating reference stories.

▶ Work with the eight-step strategy for remembering books – creating purpose and setting up your mental radar, previewing and capturing the 10,000-foot view, constructing your mental scaffolding and memorizing, speed reading for detail and comprehension, building your detailed map, creating deep knowledge through the use of memory networks and putting what you know into action.

▶ Decide on the level of detail you need to learn: for some needs a purpose, preview and mind map will be enough.

▶ Bring your skills to bear in meetings, seminars and conferences using rapid mind mapping.

14

Delivering your message: Word for word

In this chapter you will learn:
- *how to design your visual cues*
- *how to get presentations in your body*
- *how to get it right, word for word.*

What's the story

Throughout this book we have seen how creating stories can be an invaluable technique in remembering, understanding and using information. The same is true when you are presenting information, performing scripts or thinking on your feet. At the core you have to take your audience on a journey, tell them the story in a way where they can reflect on it, relate it to their own experiences, question and formulate their points of view and ultimately provoke some type of action.

The message and outcomes you want to deliver will drive your story. If it is a presentation for a new strategy, it might be an agreement on the way forward; if you are an actor in a play, it might be to have the audience experience a story from a different point of view. As you can imagine, whether you are presenting, acting out scripts or thinking on your feet, you can exploit the full spectrum of skills you are developing, particularly mind maps and creative memorization.

Mind mapping is a powerful tool for brainstorming your ideas and crafting the message of your presentation; by following through on some of the techniques described in *The four Cs* (Chapter 8), you can construct engaging presentations that take your audience on a journey and leave them with something valuable.

Action – Presenting with a mind map

Time limit: 10 minutes
Spend no longer than five minutes creating a mind map of a
60-second presentation on a topic of your choice.

▶ Practise using the mind map as a guide as you give the
  presentation to a partner or friend, or simply standing up on
  your own.
▶ Capture your thoughts about what was challenging, what felt
  good and how you might improve.

Presentations

There are whole books on the subject of giving engaging and valuable
presentations. The goal here is not to focus on presentation technique
but rather to give attention to how you can remember a presentation
in such a way that you feel you can present it knowledgeably and
with confidence.

Giving a presentation from a mind map is a technique in itself;
committing a presentation to memory is taking it to the next level.

VISUAL CUES

Visual cues are basically images or reference stories, which you usually
imagine within the location you are in at the time of memorizing.

Example

▶ *Imagine that in front of you and to the left is a bicycle.*
▶ *Imagine that directly in front of you is a very creative painting.*
▶ *Imagine that in front of you and to the right is an old, large
  storybook.*
▶ *Look at each one of these visual cues and dial up the intensity.*

These visual cues represent three chapters in this book, the learning
cycle, creative memorization and reference stories. The purpose of
these visual cues would be to guide you through three topics in a
presentation on *How to Remember Anything*.

You could create a normal memory network, but you tend to have
to look internally for this; when you are thinking quickly, there is the

potential to lose where you are. If the memory network is right in front of you, it is easy to keep track of where you are in the presentation, go off on a tangent and come right back to where you need to be. Ideally you would create a memory network in the place where you memorize the presentation and then create a similar network in the place where you will give the presentation. Details, facts or statistics connected to the presentation can be stored on any other memory network.

There are many uses for visual cues: learning sports, games, dance, cooking, physical skills – you could think of them as physical cue cards. Once you have created your presentation, visual cues are your first step to memorizing the story you are going to tell.

BLOCKING

If you are an actor, dancer or singer reading this book, you will know what I mean when I use the term 'blocking'. It is nothing to do with martial arts or boxing. It is when you map out a general plan of where you will be on stage at a particular moment; in the same way, a mind map can give you a sense of the big picture – blocking a presentation or scene can give you this same big picture sense.

When working on a presentation that has some interaction with the audience, you would physically stand up, imagine you were in the location you will be presenting with the audience in front of you and 'block' out where you would want the audience member to be when you interacted with them. Blocking out a scene can make the words that you say more memorable as you are involving your procedural and episodic memory.

While blocking your presentation you should be referring to your visual cues, using them as a guide for what is coming next: this will also start to give you a sense of what might work.

ACT OUT!

Acting out a new presentation is essential if you want to be able to present with confidence, unless of course you are an old hand and it's something you do every day or have been doing for years. The idea of Act out! is that you give the presentation as if you were doing it for real; this means if you make a mistake you don't stop, you keep going. By acting it out you are able to experience closely how it will feel *in situ* and work out any pain points. You will also find out if any of your visual cues are flaky and need to be strengthened.

Act out! can be executed on two levels:

1 Exaggerated – here you exaggerate all your physical gestures, go completely over the top, do everything with intense energy and faster than you normally would, making sure that your diction is crystal clear.

2 Natural – this is how you will deliver it on the day, live, making sure you are connecting, being truthful, telling the story and delivering the message.

Action – *How to Remember Anything*

Time limit: 15 minutes
Put together a five-minute presentation on *How to Remember Anything*.

▶ Mind map your presentation. Include:
   ▶ a personal story you can share that will help people relate to your presentation
   ▶ an interaction (memory demonstration) you would like to happen during the presentation.
▶ Create a set of visual cues.
▶ Create a table like this for your notes:

Presentation	Visual cues

▶ Block the presentation.
▶ Act out! (exaggerated)
▶ Act out! (naturally)

Scripts and speeches

The techniques used for remembering presentations can also be used for remembering a script word for word: being clear on the story you are telling, visual cues, blocking and rehearsing are all valid.

The strategy that follows aims to demonstrate how you can memorize a script relatively quickly by devising a set of visual cues that act as a framework for the words to sit upon. Once these words are implicitly embedded in memory, there will be no need for the cues as you will 'know' the script, understand the meaning and be able to deliver the message confidently word for word.

> **Insight**
>
> An actor will naturally use every part of the learning cycle, involving most if not all of their senses in the process of learning while creating emotion to experience and convey feelings. Most actors will have a method of working; there will usually be a basic framework depending on the medium. In theatre this might start with the script (sensory input); reflecting on the meaning and subtext, building a character, their thoughts, emotions, etc. (integration); questioning motivation, meaning, making choices with the director, making the director's choices fit, thinking about objectives, super-objectives and actions (integration); and finally actively testing their internal work. The purpose of this is not to try to teach you how to act but to take you through a strategy of learning scripts verbatim.
>
> There are several other careers where being able to memorize verbatim is an essential skill: lawyers, police officers, politicians to name but a few. The strategy we will go through can be adapted, depending on your style and purpose.

PREPARATION

As well as being clear on the story and message you want to deliver, it can be useful to think about what sort of perceptions you want to evoke. An easy way in is to model your speech on someone who you believe would do it really well: how would they move? What sorts of intonation would they use? This gives you a quick way to get into the speech.

Action – Speak the speech, I pray you

Time limit: 30 minutes
Following on from the Shakespeare general knowledge theme, we will use part of this speech from *Hamlet* to demonstrate the steps you can go through when memorizing scripts verbatim.

Get to know the script
Before you start memorizing, follow these steps to get to know the script

1   Read it through it and gain a BIG PICTURE understanding of it.
   ▶ What is the intention? Why are you saying this? Who is the message for?
   ▶ What is the context? Where is the scene?
   ▶ What are the emotions of the scene (keep it basic, happy, sad, angry, etc.)?
   ▶ Mind map your thoughts.
2   Thinking about Step 1: Act out! (exaggerated)

HAMLET: Speak the speech, I pray you, as I pronounced it to you – trippingly on the tongue; but if you mouth it, as many of your players do, I had as lief the town-crier had spoke my lines.

Nor do not saw the air too much with your hand, thus, but use all gently; for in the very torrent, tempest, and as I may say the whirlwind of your passion, you must acquire and beget a temperance that may give it smoothness. O, it offends me to the soul to hear a robustious, periwig-pated fellow tear a passion to tatters, to very rags, to split the ears of the groundlings, who for the most part are capable of nothing but inexplicable dumb shows and noise. I would have such a fellow whipped for o'erdoing Termagant. It out-herods Herod. Pray you avoid it.

Memorize the script

1   Create a memory network with **six nodes** in your current location.
2   Create a set of **visual cues** (make the images strong, don't memorize words yet).
3   **Connect** the cues to the nodes on the memory network.

Script	Visual cues (examples)
Speak the speech, I pray you, as I pronounced it to you – trippingly on the tongue;	A speaking **speech** (script) with a big **tongue**
but if you mouth it, as many of your players do	A line of **players** opening and closing their big **mouths**

(continued)

Script	Visual cues (examples)
I had as lief the town-crier had spoke my lines.	I had a **leaf** stuck on a **town crier**
Nor do not saw the air too much with your hand, thus, but use all gently;	A hand with a **saw** in the **air** which comes down **gently**
for in the very torrent, tempest, and as I may say the whirlwind of your passion, you must acquire and beget a temperance that may give it smoothness.	A **torrent** of rain on a **tempest** who gets caught in a **whirlwind** of **passion**, **acquires** and **begets** a nun's outfit giving her **temperance**
Script	Visual cues (your cue)

O, it offends me to the soul to hear a robustious, periwig-pated fellow tear a passion to tatters, to very rags, to split the ears of the groundlings, who for the most part are capable of nothing but inexplicable dumb shows and noise. I would have such a fellow whipped for o'erdoing Termagant. It out-herods Herod. Pray you avoid it.

4 See the visual cues and say the words aloud (connect the words to the imagery).

Consolidate

1 Block the scene.
2 Strengthen cues where needed (dial them up).
3 Act out! (exaggerate) at high speed.
4 Close your eyes, breathe deeply and let all the tension go from your body, as you start to relax. With your eyes closed, visualize the cues and whisper the script from beginning to end at speed.

Get it in your body

1 Act out! (exaggerated)
2 Act out! (naturally)

In the long term

1 Record yourself going through the speech.
2 Listen back while visualizing the visual cues and whispering the script.
3 Review after one hour, one day, one week, one month.

Insight

Interestingly I always found as an actor that I didn't think of the words as much as I did the thoughts behind the words, what my objectives were, the intention and why I was saying the things I was saying. Another useful tip is once you have memorized the script, improvise around it or say the same words as a different character: this will all go towards making the words more memorable.

On the hoof

There might be times when you have to make a presentation with only a few minutes to prepare. If this is the case, the priority should be 'What is the story?', 'What is the message?', 'What is the key outcome?'. If you can quickly get a sense of these three things, then a few things ideas will come to mind that will help you construct an *ad hoc* presentation, or will at least give you a direction of travel.

You can also take the opportunity to find out what your audience (this could be anything from a few to many) wants to get from the presentation. Start whiteboarding a group mind map and memorize key thoughts you have as visual cues in the room, mentally constructing a presentation on the fly as you head towards the outcome you decided at the beginning.

KEYS TO A GREAT MEMORY

▶ Use a mind map to pull your presentation together and help craft the message of your story.

▶ Practise the technique of presenting with the aid of a mind map.

▶ Create and use visual cues, a way of constructing a live memory network right in front of you, guiding you in the right direction.

▶ Physically block your presentation and incorporate your procedural memory.

▶ Act out! helps to create confidence in your delivery and increases memory retention, first Act out! (exaggerated) then Act out! (naturally), making the experience as close to live as possible.

▶ Master the art of word-for-word scripts, build on your presentation techniques by dialling up your cues, Act out! at high speed and visualize the scene before performing with intensity.

▶ Be prepared to make an 'on the hoof' presentation, knowing your story, message and outcome and using a temporary memory network to capture the details.

Part 4

Progress
your career

'Make your work to be in keeping with your purpose.'
Leonardo Da Vinci

15

Agile learning: The key to continuous development

In this chapter you will learn:
- *how to take control of your learning*
- *to create your learning roadmap*
- *an easy way to stay on target.*

The need to grow

The need to grow and learn is built into our DNA; knowing how to learn is an invaluable tool to have at your disposal and the strategies you have covered will set you up to do that. Knowing how to study is slightly different: study is more about planning and organizing, prioritizing, estimating how long things will take and creating rituals that help put you in a good state before you start.

Some will love studying while others will hate it; ongoing study, whether you think of it like this or not, is probably part of your everyday life. For some this is every structure, if you are a student, for example, or if you are training for a new career; for others studying happens here and there, keeping up to date with the latest in your area of knowledge.

By having a strategy for studying, you can think about your development plan: what are the things that you need to study and learn in order to meet your goals, dreams or ambitions?

Action – How do you study?

Time limit: 5 minutes
What techniques and approaches do you currently use for studying?

▶ Brainstorm for three minutes.
▶ Where could you improve?
▶ What areas of your life would benefit from further study?

Although there are many options, the method shared here is derived from a term known as 'Agile Software Development' used by many companies across the globe as a methodology for producing software, websites and applications.

Agile learning is essentially a framework that aids you in planning, prioritizing and actioning. It is geared towards continuous development and learning with a purpose. It offers a high-level view of what you need to learn to achieve your goals and is flexible enough to allow you to change that view if needed (that's the agile part). It facilitates simple planning, estimation and prioritizing of the things you need to learn that will benefit you the most.

Insight
Although there doesn't seem to be a completely consistent view of what agile learning is, the term itself has been used for a number of years. Within the context of *How to Remember Anything*, I have used an approach similar to one that has worked in the software world for a number of years, although I have shifted away from a lot of the complexities and some may say 'details', which could fill an entire book. The main benefit is that it helps to define the value in what needs to be learned, giving a view of the big picture and an easy way to plan.

Agile learning: What's inside?

There are a few terms that it will be useful to become familiar with before we look into the details.

- The learning roadmap (a high-level view of the subject you are learning)
- The learning topics (your subject broken down into topics)
- Themes (grouping of stories sometimes across learning topics)
- Stories (tasks or things to learn that add value)
- Points (number given to a story to estimate its size relative to other stories)
- A sprint (a 2-week timeboxed learning period)
- Sprint plan (short planning session)
- The sprint board (used to track progress of a sprint)
- Review (review at end of sprint)

Figure 15.1 Agile learning mind map (created using ThinkBuzan'siMindMap http://www.thinkbuzan.com).

LEARNING ROADMAP

Starting from the big picture view, your learning roadmap is a high-level view of how long it will take to complete your subject. It consists of a timeline and the **total estimated points** (this is the total points of all stories added together) it will take to complete your subject. When we go through estimating, you will see a useful way of working this out.

You can also reflect the learning topics on here. Your learning topics do not have to be studied in sequence, you will choose the highest-priority stories from across your subject for each sprint.

(continued)

Learning roadmap	Size	Jan	Feb	Mar	Apr	May	Jun
Your subject	60pts					Exam	
The brain	20pts						
Anatomy	30pts						
Memory	10pts						

LEARNING TOPICS

The learning topic is a way of classifying your subject into vertical slices; themes are a way of grouping into horizontal slices.

Example

In the example below we have a subject that has four learning topics; topics 1, 3 and 4 also belong to the same theme. This is useful when you are prioritizing what needs to be worked on in the upcoming sprint. If a theme becomes really important, you can quickly look at the stories from each learning topic that have that particular theme and see which stories from those themes make sense to learn first.

If you are using software, you can create one mind map for your subject, individual branches for learning topics, theme branches from those topics and write your stories as 'notes' attached to the branch.

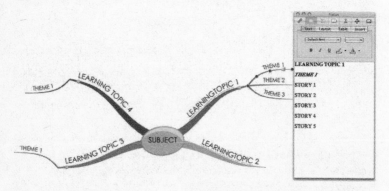

Figure 15.2 Subject mind map (created using ThinkBuzan'siMindMap http://www.thinkbuzan.com).

THE STORY

At the heart of agile learning is 'the story'. A story is basically a task, a thing to do. If, for example, you were studying to become a pilates instructor and you had to learn a programme of exercises, you would create a small story to represent that. You can write it in the way that works best for you.

Examples

- ▶ 'Learn programme of exercises.'
- ▶ 'In order to pass my exam, I need to learn the basic programme of exercises.'
- ▶ 'I WANT to learn the basic programme of exercises, SO I can pass my exam as a pilates instructor.'

Your stories will come from:

- ▶ Breaking your subject into learning topics.
- ▶ Writing your stories for each topic.

You can then:

- ▶ Group your stories into themes.

You can capture your stories in whichever way suits bests: it could be in a Word document or potentially on a mind map, as in the previous example.

ESTIMATING

Each story in your learning topic should be allocated a number to represent how 'big' you think it is; you are estimating, so it will never be totally accurate. We call that number – points.

A simple method of allocating points is to first prioritize your stories into the ones that are most important. Starting with the most important story and looking at the one below it, ask yourself, 'Is this story the same size, bigger or smaller?' Do this with each story and you will end up with a list of stories that go from very big to very small.

V. BIG		
BIG	BIG	BIG
MED		
SMALL	SMALL	
V. SMALL		

You then use a numbering system to represent your points (this can be whatever you like). This one works well: 1, 2, 3, 5, 8, 13, 20, 50.

Note: Anything over eight points is probably too big to be completed in a sprint.

Now you allocate points to the stories; the story at the bottom of the list gets a one:

If you have stories that are 13, 20 or 50 points, you will need to break them down into smaller stories just before you need to work with them in a sprint.

In order to figure out how long a learning topic will take to complete, you need to:

▶ Add up all the points from your stories within that learning topic.
▶ Work out how many points you can get through in a single sprint (you can guess or do one sprint and use that number).
▶ Take the total points in the learning topic and divide by how many points you can get through in a sprint (this will vary but you will have a ballpark figure).

Example

▶ *You have **20 stories** in **learning topic 1**.*
▶ *Let us say for demonstration purposes that each story is 2 points:*
▶ *2 points × 20 stories = **40 points** in total*
▶ *If you on average can complete **8 points** in a sprint (2 weeks), it will take you **5 sprints** (**10 weeks**) to complete learning topic 1.*
▶ *40 points in total / 8 points per sprint = **5 sprints***
▶ *5 sprints @ 2 weeks per sprint = **10 weeks***

Once you start putting points on your stories, this process becomes quite simple. In order for you to be able to create your learning roadmap, you will need to run a few sprints to figure out how many points on average you will get through in a sprint.

THE SPRINT

The sprint is a two-week study period. It consists of three phases:

- ▶ **Planning the sprint** – this is a short 30-minute session in which you look at the stories across your subject and decide which ones are most important to be worked on.
- ▶ **The sprint** – the sprint will run over two weeks (usually five study sessions a week, you can decide). At the start of each session, you ask yourself three questions that will consolidate your current learning, prime your future learning and identify where you need to get help:
  - ▶ What did I learn yesterday? (summarize it)
  - ▶ What am I going to learn today? (summarize it)
  - ▶ What are the major blockers or problems I need help with?
- ▶ **Sprint review** – at the end of the two-week session you:
  - ▶ Review everything you have learned
  - ▶ Consolidate your knowledge
  - ▶ Identify any issues
  - ▶ Decide if you need to create more stories.

THE SPRINT BOARD

Using a whiteboard is the simplest and easiest, low-tech way of planning your two-week sprints and making sure you are on target for your goals. The board summarises:

- ▶ The **learning topic**(s) you are working on
- ▶ The **sprint number**
- ▶ The total **number of points** in your sprint (add up all **stories** to be completed)
- ▶ Major **themes** and **stories** in this learning topic
- ▶ A **Pending** column for stories/tasks to be completed in this sprint
- ▶ An **In progress** column for what you are working on right now
- ▶ A **Done** column for when your story is complete
- ▶ A **burn down** chart.

The burn down chart is a simple way of visualizing your progress during a sprint. Since each one of your stories/tasks has an estimated point size, you can create a graph that has points going vertically up the left-hand side and the days in your sprint going across the bottom. As you complete a story and move it to your Done column, you deduct that number of points and draw a line.

If you don't complete anything on Monday or Tuesday, but complete a story on Wednesday, your line will go straight across for the first two days and then burn down the appropriate number of points on Wednesday.

Figure 15.3 Sprint board.

> **Insight**
>
> The sprint board shown above is actually the sprint board I used to deliver this book, although rather than learning, I was writing. The goals are different, but the concepts are exactly the same.

Your ritual

After you have your planning set up and it comes to actually putting your skills into practice, you need to make sure you get the most out of the time when you actually capture and consume information.

When you think about how you have studied in the past, do you notice any behaviours that you repeated to get you into the swing of it? How you positioned your table or chair? Whether you changed the lighting in the room? Did you make yourself food and drink? Or maybe put on some music in the background? These types of repeated behaviours can help get a person into a specific state and create some focus.

You will see top athletes with these kinds of small ritual, a tennis player bouncing the ball a certain number of times or a long jumper running through the same physical movements and thoughts before powering forward.

If you become aware of your rituals, they can become a really useful tool to get you in a state where you are ready to study.

Action – Finding your ritual

Time limit: 10 minutes

To figure out what a good ritual would look like, it is useful to remember a time when you were in the zone, when learning felt easy. If you can't think of a time like that, then a time when you were enjoying reading a book (it might just have been for leisure).

▶ Breathe deeply and let yourself relax, become aware of your body in the chair, spend some time letting yourself fall into a relaxed state. When you are ready, close your eyes and remember a time when you were learning something that felt great; it may have been from a book or being shown a new skill by somebody. As you remember that time, imagine what your perfect study space would look like. What would you need to do to set up a space that made you feel relaxed, energized and focused, looking forward to developing your skills and knowledge? What are the things you would do and say to get yourself excited about learning the things that will make a difference to you in your life?

▶ Spend five minutes creating this space in your mind and creating the ritual that will get you into the state where you are excited to learn.

▶ Once you have finished, think about how you could create a similar space in the real world.

▶ Practise running through your ritual; practise getting into the zone so you are ready to learn.

Insight

Whether you are learning or whether you are creating, a set of rituals to help get you into the right state is extremely useful. You will probably have experienced the scenario where you know you have to go and do something, perhaps write a report or learn something for a presentation or study for that exam, but you just didn't 'feel like it'. By creating rituals you can immediately change how you feel and get yourself to a place where you are ready to take action.

Although the case study is focused on a specific career, the ideas and principles can be applied to any area, be it academic, technical or vocational.

Zoe was training to be a Pilates instructor, in order to achieve this goal the subject she studies required her to pass two exams. Zoe's subject

- ▶ 1½ hour practical exam
  - ▶ Client history, Postural analysis, Outline intended focal points, Warm up, Programme of exercises suited to client's needs
- ▶ 2 hour written exam
  - ▶ 50–60 multiple choice questions covering anatomy, order of exercises, modifications to exercises with regard to postural type, muscle action during an exercise
  - ▶ 6–9 longer essay questions

Zoe's learning topics

1 Skeletal system
2 Muscles groups and their range of movement
3 Anatomical terminology
4 Planes of movement & types of movement within the planes of movement
5 Types of muscular contraction
6 Neutral anatomical position
7 Postural analysis
8 Four types of postural alignment
9 Order of exercises – 34
10 Exercise cues and modifications

Zoe's themes

For some learning topics there will be themes – for example, **exercises** are a theme that cross over several learning topics:

Postural analysis (7) and Exercises cues and modifications (10)

What this means is that in order to know which **exercises** to give people, you need to understand **postural analysis**. This is the equivalent of using symbols on a mind map to represent a relationship.

Within the learning topics and themes, Zoe has created a set of stories that represent what she actually has to learn, remember and take action on.

Muscles groups and their range of movement (2)

Each muscle has an action (movements it creates), an origin (where the muscle begins) and insertion point (where the muscle ends).

▶ SHOULDER (a muscle group)
  ▶ deltoid
  ▶ pectoralis major
  ▶ coracobrachialis
  ▶ latissimusdorsi
  ▶ teres major
  ▶ rotator cuff
  ▶ tricepsbrachii
  ▶ bicepsbrachii

Zoe's story for this might simply say:

I WANT TO *know which muscles produce which movements in the shoulder* **SO I CAN** *choose the right exercises to balance muscular issues for my clients.*

Zoe will then estimate how big this feels using points: she thinks it's about 13, which probably means it might be too big to complete in a two-week sprint, with the other things she has to learn, so she breaks it down into smaller stories and keeps this one as a reference on a post-it note, which she sticks in the Stories column of her whiteboard.

I want to know the deltoid's action, insertion and origin (2 points).
I want to know the pectoralis major's action, insertion and origin (2 points), etc.

Zoe now has the opportunity to bring all the resources she has acquired in creative memorization and put them into practice.

Insight

Zoe managed to pass her exam with an average of 93%. Using creative memorization it took her only six weeks to memorize the information she needed for the written exam. I was particularly pleased and proud as she's my wife.

Having a strategy for studying can make a big difference, whether you are working through university, learning on the job or training for a new career.

KEYS TO A GREAT MEMORY

▶ Agile learning is a framework that helps you plan your studying, prioritizing what needs to be done first, and provides a process for measuring whether you are on target.

▶ Agile learning is geared towards continuous development and learning with a purpose.

▶ The four big parts to agile learning are the learning roadmap, which gives a high-level view of timelines; learning topics, which are vertical slices of your subject and break down into themes and stories; the learning sprint board, which is your tool for keeping on track; and the sprint review, which happens at the end of every sprint.

▶ In agile learning, estimating is about working out the size of tasks relative to each other and estimating a point size that can be used to count up total points for a sprint, learning topic and subject.

▶ A sprint lasts for two weeks. Each day you should ask yourself:

  ▶ What did I learn yesterday? (summarize it)
  ▶ What am I going to learn today? (summarize it)
  ▶ What are the major blockers or problems I need help with?

▶ For effective study and a high level of performance discover your ritual.

16

In business

In this chapter you will learn:
- *what hard and soft skills you need to develop*
- *how to put your strategies into practice*
- *how to ace an interview.*

To incorporate the techniques you have explored in this book, they need to be incorporated into how you operate and for that to happen you have to start by finding 'simple' ways in which you can use these techniques that will give you a measurable benefit.

In this section we shall explore some ways that you can find that benefit and put into practice the knowledge you have accumulated thus far that can help enhance your effectiveness in a business environment.

The idea of this chapter is that it should stimulate your imagination to look for opportunities in your own life in which you can make the most of these powerful techniques.

Hard skills

In any career you will find there is a split between hard and soft skills. Hard skills may take the form of technical and academic knowledge of your job: programming if you build websites, sales techniques if you are in sales, medical knowledge if you are a doctor, vocational skills if you work as a plumber, having a physically trained body if you are a dancer or athlete. These are all 'essential' skills in order to 'do' your job; in some of these professions you may start with basic knowledge and demonstrate lots of potential to learn and be trained on the job – this is usually an ongoing process for everyone.

Previously we have looked at how to remember specific 'things'. We are going to use some 'Actions' that will help you identify what are the hard skills and knowledge you may need to learn and remember in order to progress in your chosen career. This maybe in the area you are now or something which you aspire to do in the future.

There is a clear application of the strategies in this book with regard to hard skills. Whether you are building your domain knowledge within your current role, training for new skills that will help you get a new job or career or studying within education.

The topics covered in previous chapters should give you a good understanding of how to remember technical, academic or practical skills that can improve your knowledge and application of that knowledge within your career.

Action – Identifying your 'hard skills'

Time limit: 10 minutes
Identify the hard skills you need to develop to perform at your best within your career or if you are looking for a new opportunity, identify skills for your 'ideal career'.

- ▶ Create a mind map starting with a central image of your ideal career.
- ▶ Brainstorm branches of main areas of knowledge.
- ▶ Actively daydream switching between content and form.
- ▶ Capture the skills/knowledge you would need to work within this area.

Remember this is purely focusing on 'hard skills'. In the next chapter you can refer to this mind map when building your career plan.

Action – Where can your new skills help?

Time limit: 20 minutes

- ▶ Identify to 'what areas' you can apply creative memorization and the other strategies you have acquired to become efficient with these hard skills.

▶ On the previous mind map, identify branches where you could apply your skills (you may use a symbol for this – let's say a 'star').

▶ Add branches that summarize what you would need to do (create a memory network, mind maps on research, books to read, courses, etc.).

▶ Spend 15 minutes talking through the mind map aloud, making any alterations needed.

In the next chapter you can use the insights gained here to feed into your career plan.

Soft skills

Soft skills are skills we all have to varying degrees; your ability to demonstrate these in interviews and in your career can have a big impact on the jobs you get and how you progress. In most jobs and careers there are consistent behaviours that employers are looking for; these are referred to as competencies. As you progress through your career, the expectation is that you will perform at higher levels of competency.

COMPETENCIES

The following is an example of competencies that shows a set of 'guidelines' around the types of behaviour to expect from two different soft skills. Each soft skill has three different levels – 1 is Good, 2 is Very good and 3 is Excellent.

Action – Memorizing your competency

Time limit: 5 minutes
The table below is just a template and the behaviours may not be the same at your place of work; they will most likely have their own definitions and levels.

By memorizing the competencies and the different levels you can gauge which level you are performing at.

(continued)

Communication	Reference stories (your stories)
Level 1 Clear and concise Presents point of view to colleagues Pro-active communication	
Level 2 Range of techniques to influence Adapts to situations Delivers hard messages well	
Level 3 Skilful negotiation techniques Adapts to wide range of situations Demonstrates exceptional political skills	

Creative thinking	Reference stories (your stories)
Level 1 Simplifies problems Identifies key information to support decision	
Level 2 Simplifies complex problems Gathers information and distils quickly Creative in solving problems	
Level 3 Thinks strategically Aware of the Big Picture Facilitates effective problem solving	

Other competencies include things such as teamwork, leadership, negotiation, flexibility, etc.

Insight

By running through this process for each competency in your workplace, you will have a point of reference as to where you are right now and what you need to do in order to progress to the next level. If you need to improve your negotiation skills, you may identify a whole set of training needs, books, courses, etc. for which you can use the learning cycle and creative memorization to consume, remember and put those skills into practice.

Scenarios

Now you have a good understanding of what 'high levels of competencies' look like, you can start to explore how the strategies you have learned to date can be applied in various scenarios.

For each one of these scenarios, you should think about which competencies apply and what level you would need to perform at in order to be successful.

This is by no means a full picture of how the strategies you have learned can be applied to a business scenario, it is simply some snapshots that should inspire you to look at your current and any future roles and seed ideas of how you might employ them in your own world.

MEETINGS

Whether you are with clients, in the boardroom or in the coffee shop, meetings are part of a lot of people's lives in many careers. As much as information overload, there can be meeting overload. In a meeting situation you can use the learning cycle, creative memorization, reading strategies and mind mapping to your advantage.

Action – Meetings for business

Time limit: 15 minutes
Play out each meeting scenario, identifying the actions you would take to help you be more effective.

The scenario: Off-the-cuff meetings
You meet someone outside a lift, you don't have anything to take notes on or it may not be appropriate (or you might be having

(continued)

a coffee, lunch, etc.), they tell you five bits of information that are relevant to you, maybe about the project they are working on. They also mention a person who it might be useful for you to meet. During the conversation they remember a presentation you showed them a while back and ask if you can email it to them.

INFORMATION

▶ Interested in booking a one-to-one session 30 January
▶ They mention an article about memory by Joshua Foer
▶ They are taking their pilot's licence, need help studying
▶ Belief about having a notoriously bad memory
▶ Two kids named Jill and Max
▶ John Stanton is the person who has been asking about a different type of event for his team
▶ Would like the 30-minute presentation he saw that I ran about six weeks ago.

IN PRACTICE

▶ What strategies could you apply to this scenario?
▶ What competencies come into play and what level do you need to perform at?
▶ Use the information in the scenario to practise this example.

Strategy examples

▶ *Have a set of pre-prepared memory networks available: you may have about ten of these with 20 nodes/files on each one – you will use these for random information that you receive at a time where you wouldn't be in a position to take notes. You will store the key information you hear on your memory network during the conversation, using the techniques you have learned. For each bit of information, you create your image and associate it to your node/file.*
▶ *Memorize the first five key pieces of information you hear while having a conversation with a colleague, the person's name you want to meet and the presentation you need to email them.*
▶ *Alternatively, you can create a memory network on the spot using the items around you: this can be very effective, essentially setting up some visual cues. If you are having*

> *a conversation beside a lift, start with 'items' that are on your left and cast your eyes around in a clockwise direction, picking out key items to act as your nodes/files – you can even use different parts of the body of the person you are talking to. Again, for each bit of information, you create your image and associate it to your node/file.*

Insight

When you practise this in a real situation it is useful when you create the association to ask a question about it and reflect the information back. This benefits you in two ways: first, it gives you more time to create the associations, and second, you confirm the information is correct. When you hear 30 January, imagine a MaCe (30) being swung around by a bottle of GIN (Jan) – you quickly associate that to a nearby file and ask a question, e.g. 'So on 30 January, what is the most important thing you would like to take away from this?' While they search for the information, you reaffirm your association; they will then give you some more key information – passing their pilot's exam, etc. By listening, reflecting, abstracting, asking questions and playing the information back, you are using the learning cycle to lock the information in your mind.

The scenario: Meetings with an agenda

You have been invited to a meeting in about one hour's time: there are only two invitees' names that you recognize, you have never seen the other names before, although you have an idea of which team they are in and their role. The agenda is focused on a topic that is important to you; there is some information you are unsure of. You will need to prepare for the meeting (taking into consideration 'a new way of thinking'). It's important that you get agreement on one of your ideas; you know that one of the people in the room will have an opposing point of view. When you get into the meeting, there are ten people there. Introductions are made and the meeting begins.

IN PRACTICE

▶ What strategies could you apply to this scenario?
▶ What competencies come into play and what level do you need to perform at?
▶ Think of an upcoming meeting.
▶ Go through the steps in the strategy example or use strategies of your own you have identified.

Strategy examples

▶ *Prepare for your meeting by mind mapping out the agenda, the outcomes (both yours and others), the facts that you know, areas you don't know (research these if time, or identify appropriate questions and responses), map out how you 'feel' and how others might 'feel', map out the risks and benefits associated with ideas (identifying 'who' benefits), where there is an opportunity to focus on interests between people in the room, and where there is conflict, map out potential options you could put on the table. What would your ideal outcome look like? You can use this map in the meeting as a reference, make sure you talk through the meaning of each branch out loud, or even share it with a colleague on your team to get some feedback – if you have time, you may want to create an edited version for the meeting itself.*

▶ *Research information you were able to identify and add to your map.*

▶ *Create a memory network or use one you built before and store any key facts you would like to keep in your head.*

▶ *It can be useful to memorize your ideal outcome and any facts or details associated with it.*

▶ *Look at the names on the agenda and spend a few minutes creating images for their names so you don't have to do this in the meeting – if their photos are in a system somewhere, look them up so you know who they are when you see them.*

▶ *Once in the meeting, memorize the names of the people around the table, try to do this just before it starts, so you can recap if you go around the table; this will also help build some rapport with the people you don't know and perhaps get some early insights.*

▶ *Make sure there are clear agreed outcomes at the beginning of the meeting.*

▶ *Having a pre-prepared mind map with a branch for the agenda and branches for questions, challenges, interests, ideas, solutions, agreed, outstanding and thoughts will allow you to capture 'key' information throughout the meeting. It is all right for people in the room to see these notes and can be helpful when putting your point of view forward as you can share your thinking visually on the mind map – capturing more issues, ideas and offering potential solutions.*

▶ If there is information that is relevant but that you don't feel comfortable putting on your mind map but would like to reference later in the conversation, simply store it as a key fact on your pre-prepared memory network.

▶ Use your mind map to play back what was agreed (where needed) and what is outstanding, with follow-up actions and criteria for their success.

▶ At the end of the meeting, you can memorize any key outcomes on your pre-prepared memory network that you can reference at a later date.

Insight

A key skill when influencing is being able to separate the people from the problem. By mind mapping, capturing potential feelings and hard facts, you can remain subjective and non-judgemental, making sure that you maintain rapport while being hard on the problem you are looking for a solution to.

If you spend some time on creating this ritual when preparing for meetings, you will find it takes very little time and you can hone it down into four to five minutes when needed. It will allow you to be the most effective you can be, prepared and also able to improvise when needed, and setting yourself up a framework to retain key facts that will be useful to you at a later date.

BRAINSTORMING

Whatever career you are in, at some point you will have to come up with ideas or solutions to problems, perhaps even on a daily basis.

From Edward De Bono's six 'thinking hats', we have a great model in which to utilize mind mapping in many situations and with varying numbers of people. Six thinking hats is a metaphor that allows a group of people to approach a situation or problem from the same perspective.

From a very high-level summary, a group of however many people take a specific topic or challenge and metaphorically wear the same hat; by stating which hat the group is wearing, the group can approach the challenge from the same perspective: 'Right, let's wear the white hat – everyone focus on the facts, the information we know.'

There are six different coloured hats:

▶ Blue – controls the direction of travel and focus, sets the outcomes and summarizes conclusions – one person generally wears this hat, although it can be passed around.

- White – used to gather information.
- Red – used to express feelings, both positive and negative (there is no justification needed with this hat).
- Yellow – looks for the value in the challenge.
- Black – critical (not emotional but logical and assesses negative aspects).
- Green – drives new ideas, provokes alternatives and helps to form solutions.

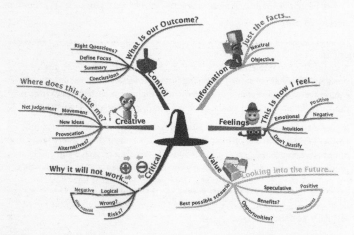

Figure 16.1 Mind map of the six thinking hats (created using ThinkBuzan'siMindMap http://www.thinkbuzan.com).

Action – Brainstorm for business

Time limit: 15 minutes
Although this is aimed at a group, you can practise it on your own. Play out the following brainstorm scenario, identifying the actions you would take to help you be more effective.

The scenario: Group challenge
You are with a group of colleagues working through a specific problem or challenge to do with your current job. There are different points of view in the room; however, it is important that you get to a conclusion in the next 60 minutes.

▶ What strategies could you apply to this scenario?
▶ What competencies come into play and what level do you need to perform at?
▶ Even though this is aimed at a group, it can work just as well on your own. Choose a problem or challenge you have and run through using the strategy examples or your own approach.

Strategy examples

▶ *Whether you take a thinking hats approach or use something a bit more free flow, mind mapping can be an excellent way of brainstorming with a group of people.*
▶ *Either lead the mind mapping brainstorm and draw on a whiteboard, or use an application such as iMindMap or Mind Manager.*
▶ *Or break the group into smaller numbers of two or three to do the initial brainstorm.*
▶ *Use a technique such as thinking hats to consolidate the group's ideas and come up with a solution.*
▶ *Pre-prepare a memory network or use the room that you are in and create one on the fly.*
▶ *Throughout the session and at the end memorize the outcomes or use your mind map as a tool to memorize the information after the brainstorming session – make sure you set time aside afterwards to do this.*

PROJECTS

There are many different applications of the techniques you have experienced so far in relation to delivering or working on projects.

To inspire your thinking in this area, consider some areas in delivering a project, the vision, roadmap, deliverables, release plan, dependencies and risks. If you have ever been involved in delivering a project or part of a project, let your mind think about where you might apply the learning cycle, creative memorization and mind mapping to improve your performance and productivity.

Action – Delivering products and projects

Time limit: 30 minutes
Play out the following scenarios, identifying the actions you
would take. There are many other areas that could benefit from
applying the strategies you have learned. The purpose here is to
identify some quick, easy wins that you can put into practice, in
your own projects.

The scenario – Planning, deliverables, dependencies and risks
You are running a small project to deliver a service or product
that you know well.

IN PRACTICE

- ▶ What strategies could you apply to this scenario?
- ▶ What competencies come into play and what level do you
  need to perform at?

Strategy examples

- ▶ *Create a high-level mind map with the four key areas:
  planning, deliverables, dependencies and risks. You could
  also include vision, outcomes, stakeholders, etc.*
- ▶ *Layer priority codes on the mind map with timings.*
- ▶ *Create memory networks for each area.*
- ▶ *Memorize key milestones, deliverables with dates and
  dependencies, risks and any other relevant information.*
- ▶ *Use the chain method to memorize your vision statement or
  elevator pitch.*
- ▶ *Memorize stakeholders, their role and their position with
  regard to level of influence vs interest. If you are in a role
  where you manage stakeholders, you will no doubt be
  familiar with the influence (or power) vs interest matrix that
  allows you to map out your stakeholders in order to identify
  the ones that are key to your project, the ones that you have
  to keep satisfied, communicate with regularly or simply
  keep informed. Knowing who these people are and how to
  approach them can make a big difference to your level of
  influence.*

LEADERSHIP

The topic of leadership is vast; in order to start to explore the application of your strategy toolkit, we can look at a small slice. From a general point of view, in order to lead, you have to be able to influence, whether that is with your peers or leading a team. In order to influence someone, you have to know already what influences them (*Creating Lasting Change*, Robbins). What are they all about, what are their beliefs, what drives them, what makes them tick? Try to understand their world and not judge it. Once you understand, you have a bigger chance of influencing and leading them to demonstrate behaviours found in a high-performing team.

In Ken Blanchard's *One Minute Manager* book, *Building High Performing Teams* (Blanchard, Carew, Parisi-Carew, 2004), he refers to the PERFORM mnemonic, in order to paint a picture of what such a team would look like:

- ▶ P – Purpose
- ▶ E – Empowerment
- ▶ R – Relationship
- ▶ F – Flexibility
- ▶ O – Optimal performance
- ▶ R – Recognition
- ▶ M – Morale

The idea is that each of these words has a set of characteristics that describe what a team would be demonstrating if they were performing at a high level. Purpose, for example, is having a common view, understanding what the vision is and why, seeing clear ways of achieving objectives.

By leading a team to meet those behaviours, you work towards creating a team that is driven, engaged and responsible for making things happen. The output of this is they strive to deliver on time and to the required specification and have a strong focus on the quality of their work and the contribution this makes to the bigger picture. Within this picture, it's also a fun place to be.

If you are currently in a team, or leading a team, think about what a high-performing team looks like for you. On a scale of 1–10, where does the team currently sit?

Action – Objectives for leadership

Time limit: 15 minutes

Play out this scenario, thinking about any experience you have had at leading or influencing people: what was your approach? What worked well and what could you have done better?

The scenario

You are fairly new to a team you have been tasked to lead. The team has gone through a lot of change and even though there are now some good opportunities on the horizon, its purpose and responsibilities are unclear, communication could be better and morale is quite low.

IN PRACTICE

▶ What strategies could you apply to this scenario?
▶ What competencies come into play and what level do you need to perform at?

Strategy examples

▶ *Mind mapping sessions with individual team members exploring their wants, needs, beliefs, values, drivers and objectives.*
▶ *Create a team memory network and memorize individuals' needs and objectives; this may even be a chain method or set of reference stories associated with the individual on a body system.*
▶ *Memorize relevant information in one-to-one catch-up sessions.*
▶ *Run workshops around the high-performing team mnemonic PERFORM; jointly create a mind map and get the team to self-rate on a scale of 1–10 (or whatever scale is suitable) where they believe they are, capturing ideas about how to improve, empowering the team to derive solutions.*
▶ *Memorize key outcomes and actions and make sure they are put into practice, utilizing the learning cycle.*
▶ *Remember the successes individual team members have and as well as recognizing them when they happen, recap within regular one-to-one catch-ups.*
▶ *Remember issues or poor performance and as well as dealing with it at the time, use this to help improve individual performance.*
▶ *Create a memory network for the team and memorize goals and objectives together.*

Interviews

Mostly everyone at some point will be involved in an interview process. With interviews there can be a great deal of anxiety and stress; in order to reduce these to a minimal level, being secure in your knowledge and your ability to demonstrate that knowledge is essential. Using your memory strategies, there are some quick wins you can put into practice that will ensure you can perform at your absolute best in an interview situation.

Action – Demonstrating high levels of competencies

Time limit: 15 minutes
You plan for demonstrating high levels of competencies; reflecting on the previous examples, identify where you can put your skills into practice and what you will gain from that.

The scenario
You are interviewing for a new role in an area that you are excited and passionate about. You have been asked to demonstrate fully the skills and knowledge required for the role.

IN PRACTICE

▶ What strategies could you apply to this scenario?
▶ What competencies come into play and what level do you need to perform at?

Strategy examples

▶ *Use relaxation and visualization techniques to 'pre-rehearse' the interview in your mind as if it is happening at that very moment, feeling relaxed and enjoying sharing your skills and abilities.*
▶ *Apply reading strategies to research valuable information about the company you are aiming to work for.*
▶ *Mind map information about the company, interviewers, your outcomes, stories that demonstrate your hard and soft skills, questions, why you want the job, why you should get it.*
▶ *Create memory networks to store the essential facts.*
▶ *Memorize stories that demonstrate your skills working through strategies in 'delivering your message'.*

▶ *In the interview, memorize the names of the interviewees.*
▶ *In the interview, have a pre-prepared memory network to capture any useful facts you may want to question later.*

There are almost endless uses for these strategies with regard to soft skills: the above five areas are just a small taster. In the next chapter you will bring together the ideas throughout this book and abstract your own view about them and focus on what benefits they can bring to your own career.

KEYS TO A GREAT MEMORY

▶ Identify what competency levels you are currently performing at and what you need to do to improve.

▶ Capture times that you are demonstrating a high level of competency and add them to a mind map or memory network.

▶ Practise using memory networks for off-the-cuff meetings and remembering details; you can also make on-the-spot visual cues.

▶ Use mind maps and creative memorization to prepare for meetings, memorizing agenda, facts and your outcomes. Memorize names during the meeting and any key facts, using a mind map to capture, reflect what has been said and summarize.

▶ Play with DeBono's six thinking hats and have dynamic brainstorming sessions.

▶ Use mind maps to plan deliverables, dependencies and risks combined with creative memorization to remember your vision and pitches.

▶ If you lead a team, think about PERFORM and how you can bring your skills to bear to facilitate a high-performing team.

▶ Be confident at interview, knowing that you have memorized key facts, competencies and stories.

17

Your career plan: Design your life

In this chapter you will learn:
- *how to identify your talents and purpose*
- *to develop smart objectives that work*
- *to condition a mindset to achieve your goals.*

There are many ways in which you can scope out your goals and career plan. In this chapter we will look at one of those options. Each section of this book has built the breadth and depth of your knowledge and given key insights and practical examples of how thinking in this way and applying it in your life can bring real demonstrable benefits. This chapter will focus specifically on how the strategies you have explored can help you progress your career.

How do you currently think of your career? Is it a job? Your work? Your mission? Your passion? How you refer to your career will have an impact on what it means to you and how you approach it.

Your purpose

In order to understand your purpose, it can be useful to think about your natural talents. Perhaps you have a natural talent to empathize, build relationships, persuade or inspire. Maybe you are driven to contribute to others, paint the big picture or be physical. It could be you are naturally gifted at forming objectives, making sense of problems or have a bond with numbers and patterns.

If you feel your current role is not in keeping with your purpose, it doesn't necessarily mean that you should jump ship. By working out what you are inherently good at, what your natural talents are, you can become clearer about your purpose and how that can help you add value to anything that you do as you work towards your ideal role.

Insight

In the 1990s, I worked in a theatre bar. The early days were not great, I wanted to be on stage rather than serving behind the bar. I knew I had to make a change as I needed the job, so I thought about what I could bring to the role. What was I good at that would help me in this situation? It was clear to me that one of my talents had always been my ability to relate to people. My purpose became *to use that talent to create a positive change* in the people I served and my co-workers. As a by-product, I became a pretty good barman, memorizing customers' names and drink orders, quick at serving and creating games with the team about getting tips. This didn't stop me from looking for my ideal role, I was still motivated to find a job that was a better fit and within ten months I was on the West End stage (in the same theatre). This purpose has remained at the core of everything I do, from actor and product manager to trainer and coach.

Action – identifying your talents and purpose

Time limit: 5 minutes

Ask yourself the following questions, creating a mind map to capture and elaborate on your thoughts. Your outcome should be to identify the things you are naturally good at (your talents) and use that to feed ideas around your purpose and where you can really add value in your personal life and your career.

- ▶ Where do you feel you have been successful in the past?
- ▶ What are the things you most enjoy?
- ▶ What are you naturally good at?
- ▶ What do you love to do?
- ▶ Where do you believe your natural talents lie?
- ▶ How can you bring your talents to bear in your current role?
- ▶ In which role do you believe you would add the most value?
- ▶ What do you think your purpose is at work?
- ▶ What do you think your purpose is in life? (If you don't know, pretend you do and think about what could it be.)

Action – Your ideal role!

Time limit: 5 minutes
Thinking about your talents and purpose, ask yourself this next set of questions to identify where they would best be put to use. Create a mind map to capture and abstract your own thoughts.

▶ What are the roles you believe you can do now, at some point in the future or would have loved to do as a child?
▶ What is the best fit for your talents and purpose?
▶ Pick out your top choice. Why does this stand out for you?
▶ Who would you be working with?
▶ Where is your ideal location?
▶ When could you imagine yourself being in this situation? (If you can't, imagine yourself 3–5 years in the future and see the scene clearly in your mind.)
▶ Mind map this 'ideal scene'.

The plan

If you have a picture of your purpose and your ideal role, you can start to look at how to make that role a reality and how your creative resources can help you get there and add real value to your everyday life.

Action – What is your story?

Time limit: 10 minutes
Mind map the high-level story of how you get from where you are now to where you want to be, highlighting what you will need to learn (in terms of skills and knowledge) and how 'a new way of thinking' can help, scenarios where you can put your memory strategies into practice, the milestones along your journey and key actions you can take.

SMART OBJECTIVES

With your high-level story in place (what you need to learn and do to reach your ideal role), you can create more detailed focus by writing some simple objectives that inspire you on your journey.

Figure 17.1

You may have come across the acronym SMART in relation to objectives; it stands for Specific (enough detail), Measurable (how will you know when it's done?), Achievable (do you think it's possible?), Resourced (have you got everything you need?) and Timed (when do you need it done by?). By designing SMART objectives, you create a clear direction of travel and criteria that demonstrate when you have arrived.

Mind mapping and creative memorization are fantastic tools for helping you to form and remember SMART objectives, so you are always clear on the targets you are aiming to hit. With your high-level story and objectives you should be flexible in the sense that sometimes you may want to move the target or pick a new one. Having them stored in your mind helps you keep track as it is easy to get caught up in the detail of your job and forget the bigger picture.

Example of a SMART objective

There are many ways to write SMART objectives: you can write them in your own style or choose to use a specific format. The following are called user stories; they capture 'who' the objective is for, what the goal or desire is and also the benefit.

As a <role>I want <to do something> so that <I get a benefit>

e.g.

As a **teacher I want to learn creative memorization from** *How to Remember Anything* **by 25 August so that I can give a presentation to my students and have them demonstrate one technique by the end of the session.**

▶ This is Specific – you know what you have to do in order to get the benefit.

- ▶ This is Measurable – you will know when you have achieved it: your students will put a technique into practice.
- ▶ This is Achievable – it's small enough that it can be done in the timeframe.
- ▶ This is Resourced – you have the book, the students and classroom equipment.
- ▶ This is Timed – you have until 25 August to complete it.

Or you could write the same SMART objective as:

In order to <get a benefit> I want to <do something>

e.g.

In order to **give a presentation to my students and have them demonstrate 1 technique by the end of the session**

I want to **remember techniques in** *How to Remember Anything* **by 25 August.**

Action – Design your SMART objectives

Time limit: 10 minutes
Using your high-level story as a target and guide, create four SMART objectives that will define what you need to do to get closer to your goal.

After each one ask yourself the following questions:

- ▶ Is it specific?
- ▶ Is it measurable?
- ▶ Is it achievable?
- ▶ Is it resourced?
- ▶ Is it timed?

PERSONAL AND LEISURE

While this plan is focused on using 'a new way of thinking' in your career, you can go through the exact same process in other areas of your life. As well as designing your career, you can play these same games to design other parts of your life, from everyday things such as hobbies you want to enjoy, to learning sports and playing games.

Mindset

One of the last elements to consider once you understand your purpose, have defined your ideal role, created a plan and have specific objectives, is how you create the beliefs that support and help you generate momentum.

In *The Body You Deserve*, Anthony Robbins gives a metaphor for beliefs, comparing them to a table top: for this table top to have any substance it must have legs to hold it up; these legs are references, memories that support this belief.

▶ If you believe that you have a bad memory – this belief is probably held up and supported by a series of past experiences; perhaps you couldn't remember facts at school, or were always forgetting names.

▶ If on the other hand you believe, not just mentally but at your core, that you have a great memory, this belief will support you in your actions and your ability to remember, as well as drive you forward to achieve your ideal role.

By actively participating in *How to Remember Anything*, you will have had a concrete experience, creating new references. You will have learned ways of remembering things you might have thought impossible in the past, forming new neuronal networks and a belief that now says, 'I have a great memory.'

KEYS TO A GREAT MEMORY

▶ Make your work be in keeping with your purpose; figure out how you can add value to anything that you do.

▶ What are your key talents and how does that map to your ideal role?

▶ What is your story? How do you get from where you are now to where you want to be?

▶ Make your objectives SMART – Specific, Measurable, Achievable, Resourced and Timed.

▶ Identify the beliefs that drive you and practise conditioning yourself for an excellent memory.

Final thoughts

Your ability to remember anything is almost limitless. You can choose to train your memory to perform at the highest of levels, or you can choose a few simple techniques that you enjoy and add some value to the things you do.

Action – Where are you now?

Time limit: 5 minutes
In the earlier sections of the book you rated your memory on a scale of 1–10 on where you were then and where you would like to be.

Where would you put yourself on that scale now?

You also benchmarked your core creative memorization skills on a scale of 1–10:

▶ Relaxation
▶ Concentration
▶ Imagination
▶ Association

How would you scale your creative memorization skills now?

The big picture
There have been a number of techniques and strategies explored throughout this book. I wanted to share with you my view of a simple picture of how it all comes together.

Everything should be done through the lens of the learning cycle: make yourself open to sensory input, make sure you reflect on the information and relate it to something you already know, look for ways to make the information your own, question it and think how it fits in with your purpose and take some form of physical action. Create as many connections as you can to the new information.

Mind mapping and reading strategies give you the big picture and the detail, employing whole-brain strategies that prime you for relevant information and make the relevant information understandable, memorable and easy to communicate.

Creative memorization is the ace in the hole, natural strategies that make the most of how you create memories. Wielding this skill will allow you to consume huge amounts of detail and facts, and create frameworks that act as the scaffolding for new information to be built on.

All these strategies combined with a plan of where they will add real value can create lasting change in your life and your career.

Use what you've learned and pass that exam, get that interview, go for that promotion, learn that new skill, make a difference to someone else and above all else, have fun.

Continuing your journey
To continue to improve your memory, I have made a short hypnosis session available that will help strengthen your beliefs in *How to Remember Anything*:

www.howtorememberanything.co.uk

If you wish to continue your journey into the fascinating and rewarding world of *How to Remember Anything*, I would love to work with you personally either at a live event or in a one-to-one session. You can keep in touch at: www.howtorememberanything.co.uk or follow @markchannon on Twitter.

Index

abstract hypothesis, *18*

abstracting, *15*, *17*, **107**, *110*, *113*, *175*

Act Out! technique, *43*, *55–6*, *57*, *98*, *186–7*, *192*

actions, *15*, *16*, *18–19*, *107–8*, *140*, *177*
    mind map, *170–1*
    see also Act Out!
    technique

active testing *see* actions

ad hoc presentations, *191*, *192*

affective memory, *31*

agenda planning, *213–15*

agile learning, *195–206*

anchor words, *166–7*

articles, *172–3*

association, *25*, *27*, *33–6*

axons, *11*, *12*, *14*

backdrops, *54*

belief, *116–17*, *229*

benchmarking, *111–12*

blocking, *186*

blocks, *105*

books, *175–80*

brain, *8*, *17–18*, *98*, *153–4*
    see also neurons

brainstorming, *215–17*

branches, *100–1*

burn down chart, *201*

business skills, *108–9*, *207–23*

capitals game, *48–50*

career plans, *224–32*

chain method, *52–60*

chunking, *64–5*, *80*

classification, *61–4*

colours, *101–2*

communication, *108–9*

communication skills, *210*

competencies, *209–11*

concentration, *25*, *30*

concrete experiences
    see senses

conferences, *180–2*

connections, *129–31*

connectors, *100–1*

conscious memory, *5*

core skills, *29–36*

creative memorization, *25–39*, *104–5*, *232*
    see also name recall

'creative state of mind', *28–9*

creative thinking skills, *210*

daydreaming, *46–7*, *51*

declarative memory, *8*, *14*
    see also explicit memory

decoding, *41–4*, *51*

dendrites, *11*, *12*, *14*

dialling up, *45–6*, *51*, *55*

directions, *133–6*

documents, *172–3*

eight-step strategy, *175–80*

emails, *169–71*

emotion, *19–20*, *32–33*

encoding, *40–1*, *51*

entertainment facts, *142–7*

episodic memory, *8–9*, *14*

eraser images, *68*

estimating, *199–200*

explicit memory, *5*, *14*, *17*
    see also declarative
    memory

facial features, *128*

filtering, *170–1*

'find the blank' game, *165–6*

framing learning, 20–1
future memory, 166–7
general knowledge, 139–62
geographical facts, 140–2
group communication, 108–9
guiding, 114–15

hard skills, 207–9
hippocampus, 8, 17, 154
historical facts, 147–9
horizontal slicing, 62–3, 80

imagery, 101
imagination, 25, 31–3
immersion techniques, 123–4
    see also directions;
    name recall; physical
    skills; prioritizing;
    repetition
implicit memory, 5–6, 14
    see also non-declarative memory
information capture, 105–6
    see also note-taking
information consumption, 106–8
information overload, 169–83
integration, 15, 16, 17–18
interviews, 221–2

journey method, 72–4

Key Management Models
(Assen, Berg, Pietersma), 74–9

leadership, 219–20
learning see agile
    learning; framing
    learning; learning
    cycle; learning roadmaps;
    learning styles; learning
    topics
learning cycle, 15–22, 95–7
learning roadmaps, 197–8
learning styles, 16, 99
learning topics, 198

lectures, 181
left brain dominant traits, 98
link system see chain
    method
listening, 128–9
literature facts, 150–2
location see method of loci
long-term memory, 8–9

major system codes, 84–9
meetings, 211–15
memory, 3–14, 18
    affective memory, 31
    future memory, 166–7
    see also creative
    memorization
memory control, 163–8
memory networks, 65–74, 92–4,
    140, 170, 177, 212
memory palace, 71–2
memory types, 4–10
mental blocks, 105
mental tags, 163–5
message delivery, 184–92
'method' acting, 28
method of loci, 65, 71–2
    see also journey method
MIN, 44, 51
mind mapping, 96–110,
    113–14
    actions, 170–1
    agile learning, 197
    conferences, 182
    documents, 173, 176
    learning topics, 198
    meetings, 214
    presentations, 184–5
    rapid mind maps, 182
    Six Thinking Hats
        (De Bono), 216
mindset, 126–7, 229
    see also priming
mirroring, 97, 102
mountains, 141–2

name recall, *125–33*, *214*
narratives, *40*, *42–4*, *51*
natural-image association, *34*, *35–6*
network building, *131–3*
networks *see* memory
    networks; network
    building
neuronal networks, *12*
neurons, *10–12*, *14*
news headlines, *174*
non-conscious memory, *5–6*
non-declarative memory, *9*, *14*
    see also declarative
    memory; implicit memory
note-taking, *98–9*
number matrices, *87–9*
number shape systems, *68–70*, *82–4*
numbers, *68–70*, *81–95*
oceans, *141*
off-the-cuff meetings, *211–12*
Olympic Games records, *157–8*
one-to-one communication, *109*
Oscar winners, *142–7*

pair game, *37–8*
paper, *100*
pattern recognition, *62*, *80*
peg lists, *65*, *66–8*
PERFORM technique, *219–20*
Periodic Table, The, *154–6*
peripheral vision, *115*
permanent numbers, *90–1*
physical skills, *136–7*
presentations, *185–7*, *191*, *192*
previewing, *113*
priming, *14*, *20*, *112–13*, *139–40*
    see also mindset
prioritizing, *124–5*, *170*
projects, *217–18*

questions, *36*, *105*

rapid mind maps, *182*
reading speed, *111–19*, *176*

recipes, *158–60*
reciting, *35–36*
    see also repetition
reference stories, *40–51*, *52–3*
reflection *see* reflective observation
reflective observation, *17–18*, *107*
relaxation, *25*, *29–30*
repetition, *7*, *123*
    see also reciting
revision, *56*
rhyme lists, *68–9*, *70*, *82–4*
right brain dominant traits, *98*
rituals, *202–3*
roadmaps, *197–8*
Roman room method, *71–2*

science facts, *153–6*
scripts, *187–91*
selective memory and minimal
    images necessary
    see MIN
self-belief, *116–17*, *229*
semantic memory, *9*, *14*
seminars, *181*
senses, *15*, *16*, *17*, *32*
seven-day challenge, *89*
Shakespeare, William, works of,
    150–2
short-term memory, *7–8*, *10*, *14*
silent reading, *116*
Simonides, *13*
Six Thinking Hats (De Bono),
    215–16
skills *see* business
    skills; core skills;
    physical skills
slicing, *62–4*, *80*
SMART objectives, *226–8*
social media, *169–71*
soft skills, *209–11*
somas, *11*, *12*
sound-image association, *34–6*
speeches, *187–91*
speed reading, *111–19*, *176*

sports facts, *156–8*
Sprint, The, *201*
Sprint Board, The, *201–2*
stakeholders, *132–3*
Stanislavsky Technique, The *28–9,
  30, 31, 32*
statistics *see* numbers
'Story, The', *199, 226–8*
study techniques, *195–6, 202–3*
subject mind maps, *198*
subvocalization, *116*
synaptic clefts, *12*

talents, *224–6*
teams, *219–20*

templates, *106*
temporary numbers, *90*
ten-day challenge, *118*
timeline technique, *165–6*

vertical slicing, *62–3, 80*
visual cues, *185–6*
visual embedding, *40, 41–2, 51*
visual note-taking, *99*

word size and font, *102*
working memory, *7–8,
  10, 14, 18*

Zull, James E., *15, 17*

Image credits

Front cover: © Duncan Noakes - Fotolia
Back cover: © Jakub Semeniuk/iStockphoto.com, © Royalty-Free/
Corbis, © agencyby/iStockphoto.com, © Andy Cook/iStockphoto.
com, © Christopher Ewing/iStockphoto.com, © zebicho – Fotolia.
com, © Geoffrey Holman/iStockphoto.com, © Photodisc/Getty
Images, © James C. Pruitt/iStockphoto.com, © Mohamed
Saber – Fotolia.com